Dallas
and
Fort Worth

FODOR'S TRAVEL PUBLICATIONS

are compiled, researched, and edited by an international team of travel writers, field correspondents, and editors. The series, which now almost covers the globe, was founded by Eugene Fodor in 1936.

OFFICES
New York & London

Fodor's Dallas and Fort Worth

Editor: Jacqui Russell
Assistant Editor: Kathy Ewald
Drawings: Ted Burwell
Maps: Burmar
Cover Photograph: Stewart Cohen

Cover Design: Vignelli Associates

SPECIAL SALES

Fodor's Travel Publications are available at special discounts for bulk purchases (100 copies or more) for sales promotions or premiums. Special editions, including personalized covers, excerpts of existing guides, and corporate imprints, can be created in large quantities for special needs. For more information, write to Special Marketing, Fodor's Travel Publications, 201 East 50th Street, New York, NY 10022. Enquiries from the United Kingdom should be sent to Merchandise Division, Random House UK Ltd, 30–32 Bedford Square, London WC1B 3SG.

Fodor's 6th

Dallas and Fort Worth

Reprinted from *Fodor's Texas*

Fodor's Travel Publications, Inc.
New York & London

Copyright © 1989 by Fodor's Travel Publications, Inc.

Fodor's is a trademark of Fodor's Travel Publications, Inc.

All rights reserved under International and Pan-American Copyright Conventions.
Published in the United States by Fodor's Travel Publications, Inc., a subsidiary of
Random House, Inc., New York, and simultaneously in Canada by Random House of
Canada Limited, Toronto. Distributed by Random House, Inc., New York.

*No maps, illustrations, or other portions of this book may be reproduced in any form without
written permission from the publisher.*

ISBN 0–679–01617–1

MANUFACTURED IN THE UNITED STATES OF AMERICA
10 9 8 7 6 5 4 3 2 1

CONTENTS

FOREWORD vii

Map of Texas viii–ix

FACTS AT YOUR FINGERTIPS 1

INTRODUCTION TO TEXAS 15

THE HISTORY OF TEXAS 20

TEXAS FOOD AND DRINK 31

DALLAS AND FORT WORTH 39
  Map of Downtown Dallas 41
  Map of Greater Dallas 44–45
  Map of the Dallas-Fort Worth Area 48–49
  Map of Forth Worth 50–51

PRACTICAL INFORMATION FOR DALLAS AND FORT WORTH 53
How to Get There 53
Telephones 55
Emergency Numbers 55
Hotels and Motels 55
How to Get Around 62
Tourist Information 64
Seasonal Events 65
Free Events 66
Tours 67
Parks 67
Zoos 69
Gardens 69
Theme Parks and Amusement Centers 70
Ranch Experiences 73
Children's Activities 73
Lakes 73
Camping 75
State Parks 76
Participant Sports 76
Spectator Sports 77
Historic Sites 78
Libraries 81
Museums 81
Music 85
Dance 86
Stage 87
Shopping 88

Dining Out in Dallas 90
Dining Out in Forth Worth 103
Nightlife in Dallas 106
Nightlife in Fort Worth 108

INDEX 111

FOREWORD

Fodor's Dallas and Fort Worth is designed to help you plan your own trip based on your time, your budget, your energy, your idea of what this trip should be. We have tried to put together the widest possible *range* of activities to offer you *selections* that will be worthwhile, safe, and of good value. The descriptions we provide are designed to help you make your own intelligent choices from our selections.

If you would like to explore other parts of this giant state, see Fodor's *Texas,* from which material for this book has been extracted.

While every care has been taken to assure the accuracy of the information in this guide, the passage of time will always bring change, and consequently the publisher cannot accept responsibility for errors that may occur.

All prices and opening times quoted in this guide are based on information available to us at press time. Hours and admission fees may change, however, and the prudent traveler will avoid inconvenience by calling ahead.

Fodor's wants to hear about your travel experiences, both pleasant and unpleasant. When a hotel or restaurant fails to live up to its billing, let us know and we will investigate the complaint and revise our entries where the facts warrant it.

Send your letters to the editors of Fodor's Travel Publications, 201 E. 50th Street, New York, NY 10022, or 30–32 Bedford Square, London WC1B 3SG, England.

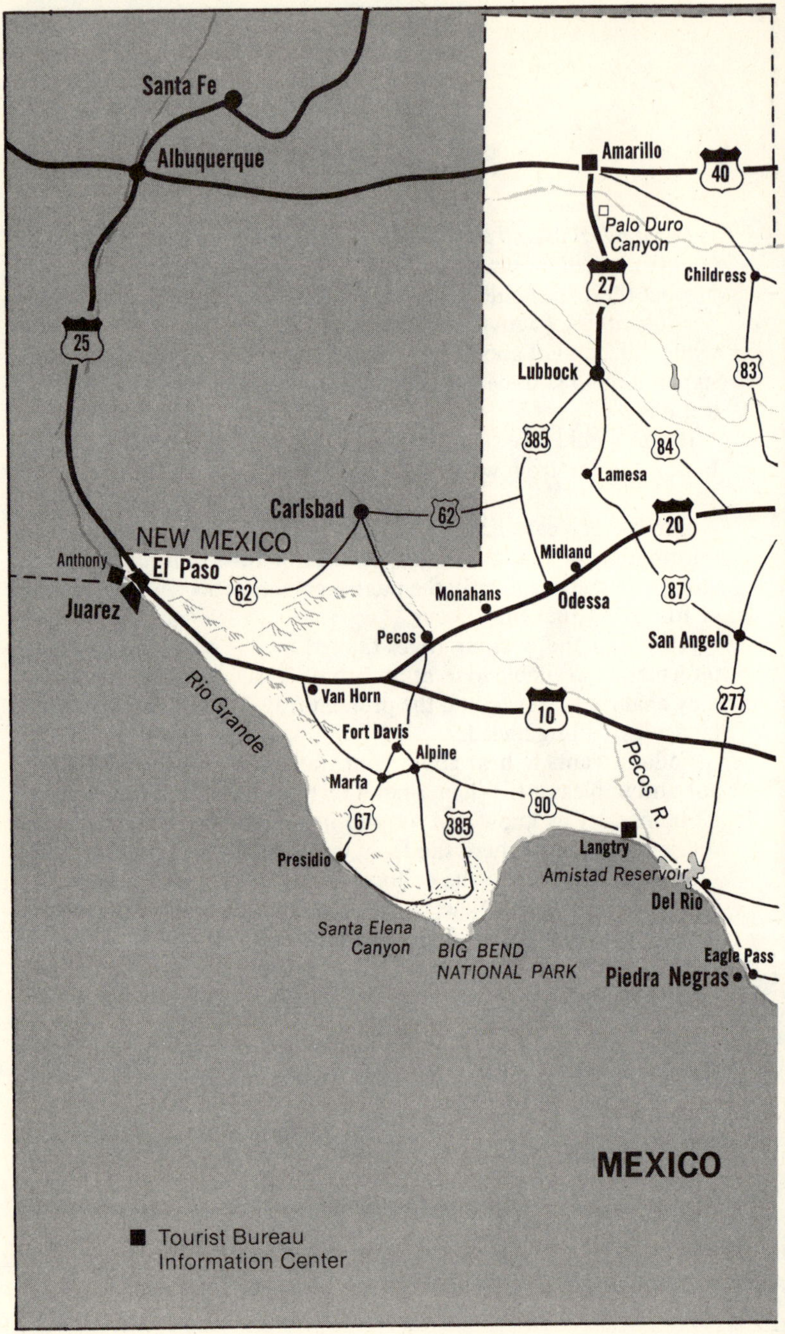

Santa Fe
Albuquerque
Amarillo
40
Palo Duro Canyon
27
Childress
25
83
Lubbock
385
84
Lamesa
Carlsbad
62
20
NEW MEXICO
Midland
Anthony
El Paso
62
Monahans
Odessa
87
Juarez
Pecos
San Angelo
Rio Grande
Van Horn
10
277
Fort Davis
Alpine
Pecos R.
Marfa
90
67
385
Langtry
Presidio
Amistad Reservoir
Del Rio
Santa Elena Canyon
BIG BEND NATIONAL PARK
Eagle Pass
Piedra Negras
MEXICO
Tourist Bureau Information Center

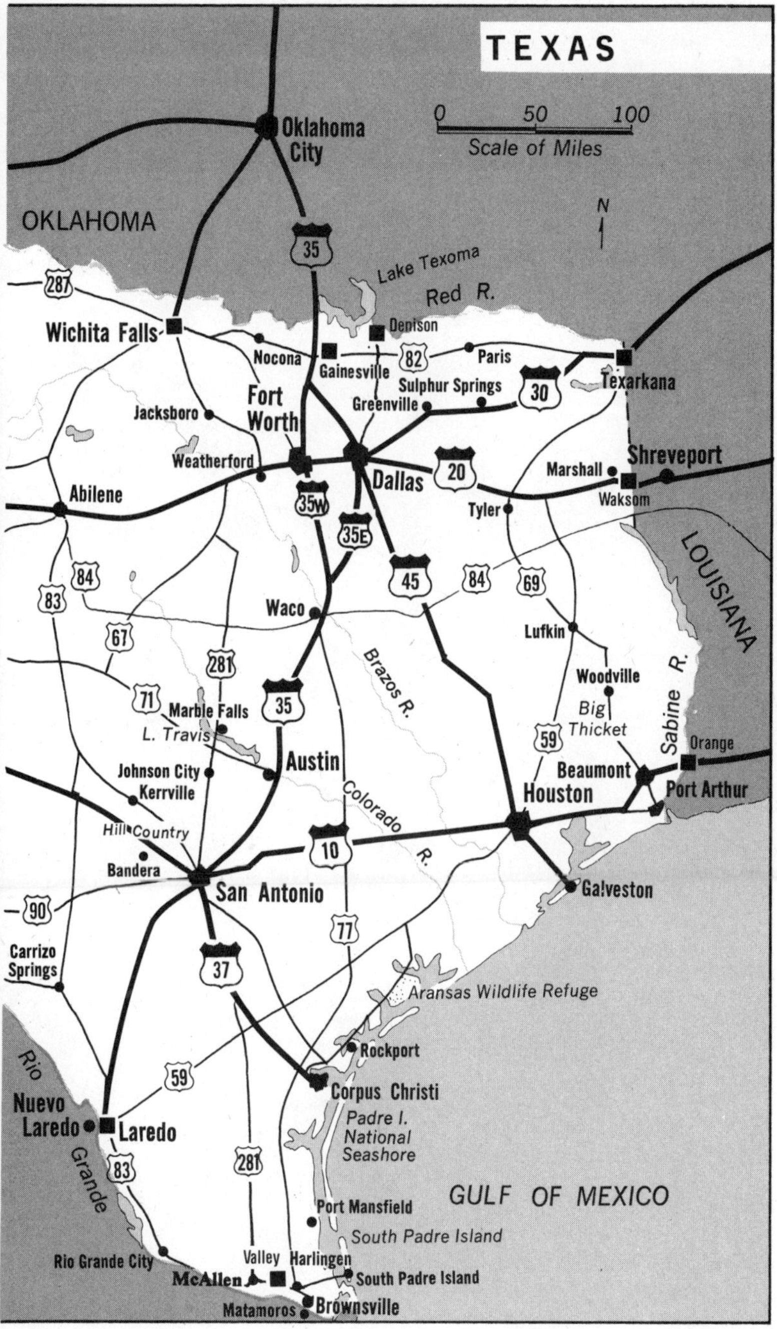
TEXAS
0 50 100
Scale of Miles
N
OKLAHOMA
Oklahoma City
35
Lake Texoma
Red R.
287
Wichita Falls
Denison
Nocona
Gainesville
82
Paris
Texarkana
30
Sulphur Springs
Greenville
Fort Worth
Jacksboro
Weatherford
Dallas
20
Shreveport
Marshall
Waksom
Tyler
Abilene
35W
35E
45
84
69
LOUISIANA
84
83
Waco
Lufkin
67
Brazos R.
281
Woodville
71
Marble Falls
35
Big Thicket
Sabine R.
L. Travis
59
Orange
Johnson City
Austin
Beaumont
Kerrville
Colorado R.
Houston
Port Arthur
Hill Country
10
Bandera
San Antonio
Galveston
90
77
Carrizo Springs
37
Aransas Wildlife Refuge
Rockport
Rio Grande
59
Corpus Christi
Padre I. National Seashore
Nuevo Laredo
Laredo
83
281
GULF OF MEXICO
Port Mansfield
South Padre Island
Rio Grande City
Valley
Harlingen
McAllen
South Padre Island
Matamoros
Brownsville

FACTS AT YOUR FINGERTIPS

FACTS AT YOUR FINGERTIPS

FACTS AND FIGURES. Texas, the "Lone Star State"—a sobriquet derived from the state flag—is known for bigness. In a state with an area of more than 2,675,300 square miles, it's easy to understand where the preoccupation with size comes from: Texas is larger than the whole country of France. You will appreciate the long distances when you drive across the state. It is 821 miles (1,321 kilometers) from Texarkana in the northeast to El Paso in the west and 872 miles (1,403 kilometers) from Dalhart in the far north to Brownsville at the southernmost tip. And to get you where you are going, there are more than 70,000 miles of highway in Texas.

But land area is not the only measure of Texas bigness. The state's population topped 16 million in 1986, making Texas number three in the nation. Texas' population is currently growing faster than that of any other state, owing largely to immigration from the Midwest and East Coast states. Today, it is not uncommon to hear a Boston brogue or a Pennsylvania dialect on the streets of Dallas or Fort Worth, alongside the celebrated Texas twang. Fifteen Texas cities have more than 100,000 inhabitants, and Dallas, Houston, and San Antonio are among the ten largest municipalities in the nation.

Because nineteenth-century Anglo settlement of Texas generally moved from east to west, the most fundamental geographical regions in the state are considered to be East and West Texas. Thick pine forests, flat, lush coastal plains, and grassy, rolling hills are most typical of East Texas; dry, wild regions and the forbidding, empty prairies dominate West Texas. But such a geographic division of the state is imprecise and can pose problems for the uninitiated. In East Texas, the term *West Texas* includes the Panhandle, the northernmost extension of Texas, which resembles the handle of a skillet, whereas in the Panhandle, *West Texas* means the area of desert and mountains west and southwest of Odessa.

For the people of the Panhandle, the top of Texas is simply the Panhandle, a vast land of high plains, endless fields of wheat and cotton, and kaleidoscopic starry vistas at night. Likewise, the term *East Texas* should include the Central Texas Hill Country, the rather mountainous and water-rich region bounded by Del Rio, San Antonio, Austin, Temple, and San Angelo. *North Texas* indicates the region around and north of the Dallas–Fort Worth metropolitan area. *South Texas* comprises San Antonio and anything south of there to the Mexican border. Thus, Dallas and Fort Worth are in North Texas; Houston, in East Texas; Austin, the capital, in Central Texas; and the port of Corpus Christi, in South Texas. Of course, any native Texan will be glad to argue with you over this breakdown of geographical regions. Go ahead; disputing is a favorite pastime in the state.

Texas is truly a land of contrasts. Mountains more than eight thousand feet high dominate the skyline in West Texas, whereas on the plains of the Panhandle's golden spread, you are sometimes lucky to spot a prairie dog mound high enough to break the uniform flatness. In East Texas are some of the thickest, marshiest forests in the nation, but the flat brush country south of San Antonio is almost devoid of high trees—though frequently almost as impenetrable as East Texas forests.

The state possesses great cultural and ethnic diversity too. In addition to the Anglo-Saxon, Hispanic, and black populations, there are longstanding communities of Poles, Czechs, Germans, Lebanese, and other more recent arrivals such as Vietnamese, Cambodians, and Haitians. Each November the Scottish clans of Texas gather in Salado for music and games. The Alabama-Coushatta Indian reservation and village near Livingston draws numerous visitors yearly. In addition, the Cajun-French influence of Louisiana extends across the border into Texas near Orange and Port Arthur.

PLANNING YOUR TRIP. Making reservations for travel and lodging can be tedious, so if you would rather not bother, use a travel agent. The services of a travel agent seldom cost a penny; the agent gets his fee from the hotel or carrier you use. Agents are helpful if you desire a package tour, in which case your pretrip planning would be minimal. If you prefer standardized hotel and motel accommodations, remember that most of the large hostelry chains publish free directories of their members' locations and special qualities.

Auto clubs are a good idea. They are helpful for itineraries, brochures, and emergency services on the road. The American Automobile Association (AAA) is a respected choice. If you live in the United States or Canada, check your local telephone directory for the nearest AAA office; if you are visiting from abroad, call AAA in the first U.S. city you arrive in. If you make your own trip itinerary, be sure the map you use is up to date. For Texas, get the Official Highway Travel Map and other information on places to visit from the state tourist agency.

Make arrangements to board the pets, discontinue newspaper deliveries, and ask a neighbor to keep an eye on your home and pick up the mail. Look into trip insurance (including baggage insurance) and be sure your other policies are up to date. Major credit cards (especially Visa, MasterCard, and American Express) are accepted throughout Texas, so plan on using "plastic" for lodging, gasoline, tickets, and major meals. Consider the safety of carrying at least half of your cash in traveler's checks, and be sure to have on hand sufficient identification (including a photo ID) to avoid undue waiting when cashing them.

TOURIST INFORMATION. The Texas highway department operates 10 tourist bureaus across the state on major highways, plus another bureau in the state capitol in Austin and one in the Judge Roy Bean Visitor Center in Langtry. The bureaus are open daily from 8:00 A.M. to 5:00 P.M. and offer the car traveler valuable brochures on Texas points of interest and copies of the Official Highway Travel Map. Their travel counselors can chart your route, give you comprehensive information about your destination, and suggest things to see and do along the way. Stop by the bureaus or write the State Department of Highways and Public Transportation, Travel and Information Division, P.O. Box 5064, Austin 78763; (512) 465-7401. Write for their book, *Texas Travel Handbook,* which includes detailed information on most Texas cities and towns—as well as lakes, state and federal parks, hunting and fishing, wildlife, and flowers, and

FACTS AT YOUR FINGERTIPS

Texas, The Friendship State, a book featuring color photographs of various areas in Texas.

For more extensive, up-to-the-minute listings of everything that is happening in the major cities, check the weekend guide sections of the major dailies. Published on Fridays, these regular sections offer weekly listings for restaurants, children's activities, nightclubs, movies, theater, sports, music, museums, galleries, flea markets, landmarks, tours and senior activities, plus a calendar of events.

Tips For British Visitors. Passports. You will need a valid, 10-year passport and a U.S. visa. You should get your visa either from your travel agent or direct from the United States Embassy, Visa and Immigration Department, 5 Upper Grosvenor St., London W1A 2JB (01–499 3443). Allow *at least* 28 days for your visa to be sent to you if you are applying by post. Note that the embassy no longer accepts visa applications made in person.

No vaccinations are required.

Customs. If you are over 21 you may import into the U.S.: 200 cigarettes or 50 cigars or three pounds of tobacco (a combination of proportionate parts is permitted), one quart of alcohol, and duty-free gifts up to a value of $100. Alcohol and cigarettes may *not* be included in this allowance but 100 cigars may be included.

You may *not* import meat or meat products, seeds, plants, fruits, etc. Avoid illegal drugs like the plague.

Returning to Britain, you may bring home 1) 200 cigarettes or 100 cigarillos or 50 cigars or 250 grams of tobacco; 2) two liters of table wine and, in addition, a) one liter of alcohol over 22% by volume (most spirits), b) two liters of alcohol under 22% by volume (fortified or sparkling wine), or c) two more liters of table wine; 3) 50 grams of perfume and ¼ liter of toilet water; and 4) other goods up to a value of £32 may also be imported.

Insurance. We cannot recommend too strongly that you insure yourself to cover all health and motoring mishaps. Europ Assistance, 252 High St., Croydon, Surrey CR0 1NF (01–680 1234) offers an excellent service, all the more valuable when you consider the possible costs of health care in the U.S. It is also wise to take out insurance to cover loss of luggage (though check that this isn't already covered in any existing home-owner's policies you may have). Trip cancellation is another wise buy.

The *Association of British Insurers,* Aldermary House, Queen St., London EC4N 1TT (01–248 4477) will give comprehensive advice on all aspects of vacation insurance.

Air Fares. We suggest that you explore the current scene for the latest on air fares, including the ever-popular *Virgin Atlantic Airways.* Texas is the hub for *Continental Airlines,* which usually has cut-rate fares for a limited number of seats on flights during off-peak times. Check the APEX fares (at press time, the round-trip on an APEX ticket cost from £367) and other money-saving fares offered by the various major airlines. Another good place to find low-cost fares is in the small ads of the Sunday newspapers and some magazines, such as *Time Out.* These fares are fiendishly difficult to come across so try and book as early as possible. If you don't fancy doing it all on your own then go to your local travel agent for expert advice.

Electricity. The current is 110 volts. You should take along an adaptor since American razor and hair-dryer sockets require flat, two-pronged plugs.

WHEN TO GO. Because of long summers and moderate winters in much of the state, the month of your visit really depends on when you *can* go. Outdoor activities that flourish during the spring and long summer include boating, sailing, cycling, golf, tennis, swimming—the list is almost endless. Of course, Texas is not famous for its winter sports— unless you consider hunting, fishing, and January golfing and picnicking as part of a winter-sports regimen. If weather is the determining factor for your trip, however, be advised that from the first of July to mid-September, the weather is *hot* across the whole state and that December through February can be quite cold in the northern half of Texas. If we consider the entire state and all the climatic zones, the best months for touring it are probably April to mid-July and October. But whatever time of year you visit, you are sure to find the sun, and definitely the fun, during your stay.

CLIMATE. Texas could be called the land of the six-month summer, May through October. In fact, the summers might be even longer were it not for the occasional early and late cold snaps that roll down from the Great Plains states in the north. Springtime is March and April, and autumn hurries by in November and early December. Mid-December to the end of February is usually all there is of winter, but even that season is temperate in the southeastern part of the state.

Texas has a continental climate, with the corresponding seasonal extremes in temperature, but the relatively low latitude and the adjacent Gulf of Mexico tend to moderate extremes over much of the state. Draw an imaginary line from Laredo, on the Mexican border, to Waco and then to Marshall, near the Louisiana line: The area southeast of the line has warm to hot, humid summer days and nights, fair springs and falls, and very moderate winters (plenty of sunny January days for golfing and picnicking).

PACKING. The easiest way to accomplish this task is to make a list for each member of the family, then check off each item as you pack it. Remember to keep accessible items you will need for having fun. Pack the film and cameras, the suntan lotion and insect repellent, toilet articles, writing supplies, swimwear, hiking shoes, sun hats, radios, maps, your guidebook, and your vacation reading material in a backpack, a kit bag, or a large purse where you can get at items quickly and easily. If you wear glasses or contact lenses, do not forget to carry spares. If you fly, be careful with your film. No matter what airport security guards may say to the contrary, the X-ray machines at the boarding gate frequently destroy photographic film.

Make sure everyone has the appropriate footwear for walking. Sturdy leather shoes or boots for the countryside and tennis or jogging shoes for urban asphalt are good choices. You might consider putting all the rain gear in one place. If a downpour strikes, you won't have to hunt everywhere for protection.

Do not take too many clothes. Nothing is more tiresome on a vacation trip than lugging around lots of heavy luggage or trying to find room in an overstuffed car trunk for things purchased on the road.

For most of the year and for most people, the heat, not the cold, will be more of a factor in planning what to wear. From March to October, the tendency is toward warm to hot days and warm, humid nights.

Women will want to stick to one or two basic colors in order to limit the number of accessories. Skirts and blouses, pantsuits and sundresses, and shorts are necessary items. For dressy evenings in Dallas and Fort Worth, take along your basic cocktail or evening wear.

Men will need ties and jackets for some big-city restaurants and clubs, but casual dress is the rule in most places. For sightseeing in the cities in summer, jeans or khaki slacks, shorts, sandals, and T-shirts are fine.

WHAT WILL IT COST? Of course, this is *the* crucial question for most of us. Gasoline and other transportation expenses are somewhat determined by your style of traveling, but they are far more subject to your destination's distance from home and the vagaries of transportation costs. Lodging and food costs, however, depend more on you, your way of doing things, and your tastes. Two people can tour comfortably in Texas for about $175 a day (not counting gasoline or other transport costs), as you can see in the table below.

Typical Daily Expenses for Two People

Room at moderate hotel or motel, including tax	$70
Breakfast at restaurant, including tip	15
Lunch at inexpensive diner, including tip	15
Drinks, dinner with beer or wine, and tip at moderate restaurant	45
Miscellaneous admissions, tour fees, movie tickets, small purchases	30
	$175

Such is a typical cost breakdown for a very comfortable trip: spacious room with TV (but no room service) and not much stinting on meals and incidental drinks and purchases. But in each of these categories you can cut cost corners and free up money for those fun miscellaneous expenses and shopping. Take lodging, for instance. There are several budget motel chains that furnish the same amenities as their more famous competitors but who do so with much less panache. The *Motel 6* chain is one frequently found in Texas. A simple, clean room for two costs under $30 a night, including tax. What do you give up? Well, maybe there is only a shower instead of a shower-bath and there is no restaurant attached. All in all, though, you definitely get your money's worth. Two more lodging suggestions are to look for reduced rates in urban hotels on the weekends, when visiting businessmen depart, and to search out motels on the old highway thoroughfares.

As for meals, why not try picnicking once a day and switching to pastries and coffee for breakfast? A portable ice cooler packed with drinks, some sandwich supplies, and a good Thermos can really dent those lunch bills. And a leisurely luncheon in a city or roadside park can be more relaxing than sitting in a busy restaurant. Just make sure to keep your picnic kit accessible in the trunk.

HINTS TO THE MOTORIST. Because of the fine highways, a wide variety of landscape, and limited rail and bus routes, traveling by motor car is definitely the best way to see Texas.

Although sometimes you may doubt it, Texas observes the 65-mph (89-kph) speed limit (except, of course, where otherwise indicated). A large anti-55-mph lobby exists in the state, because there are such long distances between the cities. Remember, it is almost 1,000 km. from Houston to Amarillo and more than 1,200 from Houston to El Paso. But the lobby won't help you if you exceed the limit and are stopped by a Texas Department of Public Safety officer. Keep to 65 mph unless lower speeds are posted. Traffic fatalities have decreased since the nationwide speed limit was instituted.

Lower speed limits are enforced in communities. Watch for signs saying "Speed Zone Ahead" and be prepared to decelerate. Keep alert when driving on weekdays during the school year (August-June); school zones are usually marked with flashing yellow lights and permit only very low speeds. And if you find yourself behind a loading or unloading schoolbus, don't pass or overtake it—it's against the law. Of course, you will encounter few speed zones and schoolbuses on interstate highways and urban expressways.

Before leaving home, have your regular mechanic thoroughly check your car. It might be wise to join an auto club that renders emergency and repair services on the road, or to investigate your auto insurance to see if you are covered for towing and emergency charges. While you are doing that, make sure your insurance policy is in force and take proof of that fact with you.

If you need repairs en route, look for a garage displaying the National Institute for Automotive Service Excellence (NIASE) seal. You may need to check the Yellow Pages of the local telephone directory for auto-parts stores that are open 24 hours a day; quite a few cities have them. But if it is Sunday, you're far from a metropolitan area, and you need that fuel pump or special fan belt for your disabled car, your chances for fast service are slim. To avoid such a scenario, carry some emergency parts and tools in the trunk of your car, along with the jack, the spare tire, and your jumper cables.

Locating gasoline is rarely a problem. If gas stops are few and far-between on a U.S. or a Texas state highway, road signs will indicate the distance to the next service station.

Texas maintains a splendid system of interstate, U.S., and state highways, with an aggregate length of more than 70,000 miles. You will find that your pleasure and knowledge of the land will be increased if you drive some of the many farm-to-market and ranch roads that crisscross major routes. Most of these secondary roads are comparable to regular two-lane, shouldered highways in other states. So if you have the time, be adventurous. Take a few of these not-so-well-traveled roads. For a detailed map of all Texas highways and roads, pick up the Official Highway Travel Map from one of the Texas tourist bureaus. "F.M." means "Farm-to-Market Road," and "R.M." means "Ranch-to-Market Road."

TRAILERS

Towed vehicles or trailers more than 55 ft. (16.8 m.) long or 8.6 ft. (2.44 m.) wide require special permits in Texas. The permits are good for single trips, from points of origin to destinations, not exceeding 15 days. The $10 fee is payable by cash, cashier's check, money order, Mastercard, or Visa, and you must supply the license number, make, model, and weight of the trailer, plus the license and engine numbers of the towing vehicle. The permits are available from any State Department of Highways and Public Transportation district office and from the Texas tourist bureaus (see *Tourist Information,* p. 2), or call the Central Permits Office in Austin at (512) 463-0241, or (800) 227-6839.

WHAT TO DO WITH THE PETS. Will you take your pet dog or cat on the trip? More and more motels accept them now. Check before you register. If this is your first voyage with your pet, accustom the animal to car travel before you leave. Don't let a dog ride with its head out the window; wind, sand, dirt, and gravel might damage its eyes permanently. Just crack the glass enough for his nose. See that the pet exercises regularly. Highway comfort stations and rest stops are excellent places to halt for a spell and unwind, and many have the bonus of being scenic. Don't forget your pet's water and food dish. And never, never leave a dog or cat in the car on a hot day, even with the window cracked open. The blazing Texas sun can heat the inside of a car to more than 115°F. (46°C.) in a matter of minutes.

HOTELS AND MOTELS. *General tips.* Always make advance reservations whenever possible. Otherwise, you are sure to waste time and energy at least once in your trip looking for accommodations that, in the end, may not suit your needs. If you don't have reservations for the night, start looking for a hotel or motel early, say four o'clock. Remember that special sporting or cultural events of which you are unaware may cause all the vacant rooms in a city to disappear on a certain day—the day you might arrive in town without a reservation. During the football season (Sept.–Jan.), floods of weekenders descend on Dallas–Fort Worth.

When you make advance reservations, advise the hotel or motel operator when you expect to arrive. Most hostels will not keep reservations after 6:00 P.M., so if you want to be absolutely sure to have a room when you arrive late, give the number of one of your credit cards over the phone to pay for the lodging in advance. Many chain or associated motels and hotels will make reservations with their affiliates at your next destination.

Whether to choose a hotel or a motel for your lodging is a difficult decision, since the amenities in each category are so similar. But in general, you will find that hotels offer a bit more personalized service to their guests. Also (in general) hotels run a bit more expensive than motels of comparable quality. Many hotels have one-day laundry and dry-cleaning service, whereas motels are more prone to offer a coin-operated laundromat, if anything. Room service is rare in motels but almost always available in hotels. Seldom, if ever, do you have to pay for parking at a motel; in hotels, there is usually a charge for use of the hotel garage, in addition to the tip you give the parking attendant. You won't find porters and bellmen in motels (unless you are in a resort area), but, on the other hand, you will probably be able to park quite near your room. Television, bedside telephones, and in-room toilets, baths, and showers are standard fare for motels and hotels in all price categories. Many have swimming pools, even in downtown areas. As for motels and motor inns in the urban areas, you will find that they offer about the same conveniences as the older, sometimes more elegant hotels, the only exception being more personalized service in hotels.

Hotel and motel chains. In addition to the hundreds of fine independent motels and hotels in Texas, many lodging establishments belong to national or regional chains. Two advantages to staying in chain motels are the ease of making future reservations and the great degree of standardization among the affiliates. You know almost exactly what kind of room you will have tomorrow night by looking at the one you have tonight. The main hotel chains in Texas are *Hilton Inns, Hyatt, Marriott,* and *Sheraton.* The major motel chains are *Best Western, Holiday Inn, Howard Johnson's, La Quinta, Quality Inns, Ramada Inns, Days Inns,* and *TraveLodge.* In all the hotel and motel chains mentioned above, you can expect at the least to find rooms with full baths, color TV sets, telephones, desks, carpeting, and usually double or queen-sized beds. Budget motel chains also exist in Texas, and they offer almost the same amenities (right down to the swimming pool) but at a substantial savings. Two economical chains worth mentioning are *Rodeway Inns* and *Motel 6.*

Categories. Hotels and motels in all the Fodor's guidebooks to the U.S.A. are divided into five categories, arranged primarily by price but also taking into consideration the degree of comfort, the amount of service, and the atmosphere that will surround you in the establishment of your choice. The dollar ranges for each category are clearly stated before the listing of establishments for each city. Remember that prices and ratings are subject to change on rather short notice. We should also point out that many fine hotels and motels had to be omitted for lack of space.

Super Deluxe. A category reserved for only a few hotels that render deluxe accommodation in a special atmosphere of glamour, good taste, and dignity. The hotel will probably be a meeting place for local high society. The tops in everything, including price.

Deluxe. The minimum facilities must include bath and shower in all rooms, suites available, a well-appointed restaurant and bar, room service, color TV and telephone in room, air conditioning and heat, and ample personalized service including laundry service if it is a hotel. In a deluxe motel or motor inn, fewer services may be available by employees and more by automatic machines.

Expensive. All rooms must have bath or shower, TV and telephone, attractive furnishings, and heat and air conditioning, and there must be a restaurant within or next door to the establishment. Motels in this category may have laundromats, which should be in a convenient location.

Moderate. Each room will have a bath or shower and (unless in a resort area) TV and a telephone; a restaurant or coffee shop should be nearby. Functional lodging, perhaps not in the best location.

Inexpensive. Almost always the rooms will have a bath or a shower, but occasionally such facilities might be down the hall. TV and telephone may be included, optional, or unavailable. Clean, functional rooms are the minimum. In *Motel 6* and *Rodeway* there is always a pool. Motels in this price range are usually good bargains; in hotels you might want to look over the room before you take it.

DINING OUT. Except for a few fancy establishments in Dallas and Fort Worth, evening meals are the only ones for which you should occasionally worry about reservations. To make matters complicated, more and more restaurants refuse to accept reservations, preferring instead to have you sit in their bar or lounge drinking expensive liquor until a table is ready. On a busy night (Friday, Saturday, Sunday) you should call up before leaving your hotel and ask how long a wait there will be before getting a table. Seven o'clock is usually when the largest crowd arrives.

Texas is a state for casual dress. Few are the restaurants where a man would be turned away for want of a tie. "No shoes, no shirt, no service" is a much more common warning to customers than "Gentlemen need jackets." Women should encounter even fewer problems as long as they don't wear shorts or jeans to a swanky restaurant in Dallas or Fort Worth. If you are traveling with children, you may want to call ahead to a restaurant to see whether it offers a children's menu. Lower-priced plates for kids are rapidly disappearing.

Restaurant Categories. Restaurants in Dallas–Fort Worth are classified in this volume according to type of cuisine served and the price for a typical meal (without extras). Limitations of space make it impossible to list every establishment. Instead, you will find what we consider to be the best selections in each category. As a rule, prices in metropolitan areas are higher than those in rural regions. Although the various restaurant categories are the same throughout the Fodor's series of guides, the prices in each category may differ from region to region. You will see the dollar ranges for each category clearly stated before the listings of the restaurants. Menus are volatile; prices might go up after press time. In all our categories, the price range *does not* include cocktails, wines, cover charges, tips, or extravagant house specialties.

Deluxe. This category denotes an outstanding restaurant with a lavish or particularly attractive atmosphere. These restaurants are indeed difficult to get out of for less than $25–$30 per person, even if you skip dessert and alcohol and order the cheapest thing on the menu. Deluxe restaurants should have a superb wine list and a good bar, excellent service, and delectable food.

Expensive. In addition to the expected dishes, an expensive restaurant will offer one or two house specialties, a good wine list, cocktails, air conditioning, good service, and a good atmosphere for dining in comfort.

Moderate. Cocktails or beer available, air-conditioned, better-than-average service, and a reputation for wholesome food.

Inexpensive. Good food at bargain prices. Frequently there are house specialties, too. Availability of beer, wine, and drinks may vary. Air conditioning, tables (or tables and counter), good service.

TIPPING. Giving tips expresses your appreciation for service well received. You should reward courteous, efficient service fairly. Likewise, when you receive poor or surly service, you should express polite dissatisfaction by reducing or withholding your tip. In many service establishments, especially restaurants, waiters and waitresses are paid far below the prevailing minimum wage. Much of their income depends on the tips they receive. This system is intended to induce good service. But we, as customers, must remember that courteous and efficient service is all that should be required for an employee to receive the standard gratuity. A waiter can render extra-special attention to your desires only if that attention is not at the expense of other customers. When you get such special attention, it merits extra compensation.

The standard tip for restaurant, bar, and cocktail-lounge service is 15% on the amount of the bill *before* taxes. Do not include the tax when figuring your tip. Good service, however, might be more easily rewarded by simply dividing the pretax amount by six and then rounding off to the nearest quarter. This calculation provides a tip of about 16.7% and is often quicker to determine than figuring exactly 15% when you're in a hurry or if you're not an arithmetic whiz. Similarly, if service was not quite up to par, dividing the pretax amount of the bill by 8 or 9 will render 12.5% or 11.1%. You can be assured that the difference will be noted by the employee. In many Texas establishments, a service charge (usually 15%) is included in the bill for parties of six or more. When it is, an extra 5% tip is necessary only if you made many special requests or if you genuinely appreciated the waiter's attention. When you drink something at a bar or at the counter in a restaurant, leave at least 10% (25¢ minimum). There is no tipping in fast-food restaurants, self-service eateries, and outdoor concession stands.

A hotel bellman gets 50¢ per suitcase, unless you load him down with a lot of extras. If you do, give that extra $1 or $2. Doormen and parking attendants usually receive $1 for parking or fetching a car. For short stays in hotels and motels it is not necessary to tip the maid unless you throw a party in your room or make a mess. If you stay longer than two nights, leave the maid about $1 a day, on the last day of your stay. Room service gets about 15% of the bill before tax (but be sure to check the bill first for any included service charge). Tip barbers and hairdressers 10%, minimum $1. The person who washes your hair gets 50¢ (unless it's the barber or hairdresser who does it). Manicurists get 10% of their bill, and so should shoeshiners.

Tip 15% on taxi fares. If the driver helps you with your luggage, give 25¢ per item for loading and unloading and 50¢ per item if he helps you carry them any distance. On the train, give 15% to dining-car waiters and $1 a night to the sleeping-car attendant. Remember, there is never any tipping on a plane. Tip airport porters and redcaps the same as hotel bellmen for carrying your luggage.

SENIOR-CITIZEN AND STUDENT DISCOUNTS. Since there is no uniformity in age-related discounts, the only thing to do is to ask each time you purchase an admission. Some attractions in Texas—especially museums, cultural spectacles, and movie houses—offer discounted admissions to senior citizens (generally 65 and older) and to bona-fide students. Some proof of age and affiliation will be required. Usually, places offering student discounts will be more strict—they may require a high school or college ID or possibly an international student travel card. Most cinemas now require the student to provide proof of age and then to purchase a special student pass in order to get student admission at that theater. Few, if any, discounts remain for air, rail, or bus tickets. One place to look for special senior-citizen rates and privileges, though, is the state and national parks.

DRINKING LAWS. The minimum age in Texas for consumption and possession of alcoholic beverages is 21. Other liquor laws vary from county to county. Out of 254 Texas counties, 69 are wholly dry—that is, no alcoholic beverages are sold. In 14 counties, only beer or beer and wine are marketed. In 171 counties, which include all the major cities, the status is wet, at least in part.

Bottled distilled liquor must be purchased in state-licensed package stores, which may be open from 10:00 A.M. to 9:00 P.M. except on Sundays and certain holidays. Beer and wine can be bought in liquor stores, supermarkets, and convenience stores between 7:00 A.M. and midnight, except on Sundays, when beer and wine sales begin at noon.

BUSINESS HOURS, HOLIDAYS, AND LOCAL TIME. Dallas and Fort Worth, like most of the rest of Texas, are on Central Standard Time from the last Sunday in October to the last Sunday in April. (CST is the same as Chicago: one hour earlier than New York and the East Coast, six hours earlier than GMT.) El Paso is on Mountain Standard Time, one hour earlier. As in the rest of the United States, on the last Sunday in April the clocks are advanced one hour to establish Daylight Savings Time. On the last Sunday in October, they are turned back an hour.

Texas banking hours are generally from 9:00 A.M. to 2:00 P.M., but you can usually find "mini-lobbies" and drive-in windows in major banks that are open before and after the main-lobby schedule. Most large banks operate their drive-in facilities on Saturday, too. Remote self-service stations are now being used by banks; these require bank or credit cards and are accessible 24 hours a day seven days a week in most shopping centers and some grocery stores. Currency-exchange services are found only in the larger banks in the main cities, so be sure to change foreign monies in sufficient amounts or carry your funds in U.S.-dollar traveler's checks.

Shops and boutiques usually open at 8:30 or 9:00 A.M.; department stores and shopping malls, at 10:00. Many malls, and some stores, stay open until 9:00 P.M. Otherwise, the closing hour is generally 5:30. Most professional offices, businesses, and government bureaus open at 8:00 A.M. and close at 5:00 P.M..

The banks, most businesses, and some restaurants are closed on the following holidays: New Year's Day; Presidents Day, mid-February; Easter; Memorial Day, end of May; Independence Day, July 4; Labor Day, early September; Thanksgiving Day, late November; and Christmas, December 25. The banks and some other establishments are also closed on Columbus Day in mid-October and Veterans Day in early November. Texas state holidays are also celebrated, but they usually affect only state-government offices. Texas Independence Day, a big hoo-ha, is March 2nd.

POSTAGE. Don't forget that U.S. domestic airmail rates apply to Mexico, too. The current first-class rate is 25¢ for letters of 1 oz. (28 g.) or less and 15¢ for postcards. Letters to Canada cost 30¢; postcards cost 21¢. To all other destinations in the world the rate is 45¢ for letters and 36¢ for postcards. International aerogrammes cost 40¢—but do not enclose anything in them.

SPORTS. Participant Sports. If you enjoy knocking little white balls around beautiful countryside, don't leave your **golf** clubs behind when you visit Texas. There are municipal courses and golf clubs galore all across the state: courses with forest-lined fairways and deep water hazards in East Texas; with rolling hills and tight doglegs in the Hill Country; and with wide-open, long, straight par-fives in the Panhandle. In Far West Marfa, you can play on a mile-high municipal course while sail planes soar on thermal currents far overhead. Many Texan golfers choose an area of the state and play every course in it for their vacation relaxation. The Hill Country, the Rio Grande Valley, and the region around Austin are good for such intensive encounters with your handicap. True championship courses are found in Fort Worth, San Antonio, Houston, Austin, The Woodlands, Horseshoe Bay on Lake LBJ, Lakeway (a Jack Nicklaus course on Lake Travis), and Dallas.

Texans are into **tennis** in a big way. Several pros have come from Texas, and several still live there. Championship municipal courts and clubs abound in Dallas–Fort Worth, but for casual exercise you can find free courts in almost any public park. Some state parks also have courts.

Racquet ball is becoming popular, and more and more private courts in fitness centers are being built. Supreme Courts is a widespread chain. Squash courts are more difficult to find. Check for courts at institutions of higher education. You might be permitted to play for a fee.

Runners should definitely bring their togs and shoes. Texas can boast of many scenic and manicured hike and bike trails. **Bicycling** is also gaining ground every year in Texas, especially in the cities. Of course, **horseback riding** is popular in the most cowboy of all states. Western-style riding prevails. English riding, show riding, and steeplechase are found only in or near the largest cities, and without an invitation you may be limited to being an onlooker.

Spectator Sports. One word that just about sums up this category is **football.** From August to the end of January, the football fever runs amok in the state. During your trip you can measure just how passionate and serious a disease this is by counting the bumper stickers praising the Dallas Cowboys, the Houston Oilers, or any of the hundreds of university and high school teams. College football season runs concurrent with the professional schedule. Most of the Southwest Conference football teams are based in Texas. For some real Texan excitement around a real American experience, take in a game in one of the enormous stadiums bedecked with Astroturf and bright lights. It is unforgettable.

Baseball follows football today as the most popular spectator sport, but it is still the most all-American one. Professional games are held in Dallas and Houston. Good college encounters can be found during the spring.

Rodeos are held regularly in both large and small communities all over the state. Check local newspapers and magazines for times and locations. If you are visiting Dallas, you can take in a rodeo in nearby Mesquite on any Friday or Saturday from April to September. Year-round rodeos are held at 8:00 P.M. Saturdays at the Roundup Rodeo in Simonton (west of Houston) and KowBell Rodeo in Mansfield (south of Dallas–Fort Worth).

CAMPING AND RV FACILITIES. Camping facilities are widespread in Texas, and more are springing up each year. National parks, state parks, municipal parks, as well as private firms and individuals, provide campgrounds for tents and hookups for recreational vehicles.

Of 90 state parks and monuments across Texas, half of these have at a minimum electricity and water hookups, restrooms, and cooking facilities, and some of those also have sewage hookups and showers, swimming pools, and tennis courts. Hookups cost an additional fee of about $5 to $7 a day. Reservations for camping spots in state parks are strongly recommended, especially during the summer.

Municipal parks in Dallas–Fort Worth also provide limited camping and RV facilities. If you are unsure whether a municipal campground is situated in a city, call the local chamber of commerce tourist bureau or refer to the municipal listings in the blue or Yellow Pages of the phone book.

Private campgrounds and RV parks are often small and here-now-gone-tomorrow enterprises. That is not to say that they offer fewer or poorer services, just that they are more difficult to locate. Look for private campgrounds near the state parks and recreation areas, since their private counterparts will be trying to capitalize on the excess of visitors to the parks. One chain campground that is an exception to this is *Kampgrounds of America* (KOA), a series of well-maintained RV and camping parks near recreation areas and cities. For more information, write KOA, Inc., P.O. Box 30558, Billings, MT 59114, or check the local phone book for a nearby listing. KOA grounds often have grocery stores, telephones, and swimming pools.

For more camping information, you may want to contact a Texas tourist bureau (see *Tourist Information,* p. 2) to get a copy of the *Texas Public Campgrounds Guide.*

THEME PARKS. *International Wildlife Park,* between Dallas and Fort Worth, off I-30, is a drive-through game preserve of African animals brought to Texas for protection and breeding. Its entertainment "village" offers a petting zoo and rides. Open daily late April to late September, weekends spring and fall.

Six Flags over Texas, between Dallas and Fort Worth, off I-30, is 200 acres of blended history and fantasy, set against the half dozen sovereign flags that have flown over the state. The admission ticket lets you enter 100 rides, shows, and exhibits. Food, souvenirs, and a gaming arcade are available. Open weekends in March, April, and September through November; daily from mid-May to Labor Day.

For other theme parks, see the *Practical Information for Dallas and Fort Worth* sections of this book.

HINTS TO HANDICAPPED TRAVELERS. All federal and state and most city office buildings; the state universities, colleges, and parks; and most municipal street departments have instituted, or are in the process of instituting, special privileges and facilities for the handicapped. More and more curbs, especially in downtown areas, have antislip ramps for wheelchairs. Reserved parking spaces are often seen. And public bathrooms and toilets have special stalls. Most businesses have been following suit.

Many hotel and motel chains, including *Holiday Inn, Hyatt, Ramada,* and *Sheraton,* have made efforts to provide special rooms for the handicapped in most of their establishments. Be sure to ask the hotel or motel if they have special accommodations when you call to make reservations.

Many state parks have paved, level nature trails that easily accommodate handicapped visitors. Call the individual park before your visit, to find out for sure. For travel tips for the handicapped, write the following organizations: Consumer Information Center, Pueblo, CO 81109; Society for the Advancement of Travel for the Handicapped, 26 Court St., Suite 1110, Brooklyn, NY 11242.

Access to the National Parks is a handbook that describes facilities for the handicapped at all national parks. It costs $3.50 and is obtainable from the U.S. Government Printing Office, Washington, D.C. 20402. For a free copy of *Access Amtrak,* a train guide for the handicapped, write Amtrak, National Railroad and Passenger Corporation, 400 N. Capitol St., N.W., Washington, D.C. 20001.

INTRODUCTION TO TEXAS

by
MOLLY IVINS

Molly Ivins is an East Texan who has been in the newspaper business for twenty years, including a stint as a correspondent for The New York Times. *For six years she was editor for the* Texas Observer, *and she is currently a columnist for the* Dallas Times-Herald.

Texans are actually just like everyone else in this country, only more so. That's why John Bainbridge called his book about us *The Super-Americans.* Everything that is good and, I regret to report, most of what is bad in America exists in Texas in an exaggerated form. I don't know why the state has this slightly larger-than-life quality. I suspect it has something to do with a lack of self-consciousness; for some reason, Texans almost never worry about making fools of themselves.

Let me confess right away that I love Texas passionately; but I regard that as a harmless perversion, and I discuss it only with consenting adults. I cannot promise you will see "my" Texas as you wander through this exuberant, uproarious nation-state. But I urge travelers to approach it the way a good Texan approaches an adventure. You may learn much here about history, different cultures, and racism; you will see glorious natural beauty and architectural wonders; and for all I know, you may suffer self-improvement as a result. But if I were you, I'd come to Texas just for the fun of it. Let 'er rip. EEE-YAH!

Texas—I believe it has been noted elsewhere—is a big state, and in it are any number of symptoms of civilization: symphony orchestras, theater companies, museums, universities, poets, scholars, and fern bars. But I think what makes Texas Texas is more in the EEE-YAH! vein. Texas is a wonderful, funny, and astonishing place, but it helps if you are not afflicted with excessively refined sensibilities. Texas can be tacky.

The state is considerably more complicated than its Hollywood stereotype. Geographically and economically, it can be divided into five separate and distinct regions. It is also a mosaic of cultures; the pieces of the mosaic overlap from one region to the next, and the darker ones always wind up on the bottom. The cultures of Texas are black, Hispanic, southern, standard suburban, and kicker (short for shitkicker). The kickers are the most obvious.

Kickers used to be mostly country people, but the combination of migration to the cities and the spread of the drugstore-cowboy culture has erased that distinction. Nowadays, kickers are more likely to be refinery workers, insurance salesmen, or secretaries than real cowboys.

There used to be a great animosity in Texas between the freaks and the kickers. Twenty years ago, if a longhair wandered into a kicker bar by mistake, he was apt to have his carcass stomped. All that has been radically changed by the most revered artist in Texas, Willie Nelson, the great singer and composer of progressive country music. Willie is a longhair his own self, and those two cultures somehow got married around his music: The kickers took to letting their hair grow and the longhairs turned in their sandals for boots, and now it's kind of hard to tell one from the other.

The redneck tribes of Texas are identified by certain distinctive totems; pick-em-up truck with guns slung across the back window racks is a solid clue. Drivin' down the highway real fast, throwin' beer cans out the window while country music plays real loud on the radio is also a giveaway. Necks are noted for gettin' drunk on Saturday nights, usually makin' it to church Sunday mornin', and tellin' Rastus-and-Liza jokes. Most everybody in the whole state loves football, country music, and beer.

Texans are not particularly civilized people; they shoot, knife, and stomp one another to death with some frequency, and they fight in bars on occasion. They're slightly obnoxious to be around when they're having fun. They laugh real loud, hoorah a lot, bang their beer bottles on the table, and just do carry on. They do not shout when they get mad, and they tend to get very quiet just before they become violent. That's when you should leave the bar. Texans are a great deal like Aussies—they cuss a lot, drink enormous quantities of beer, and don't put up with much . . . uh . . . guff.

By way of compensation, we are a notably friendly lot. There is, of course, no way to prove this, but it is my own observation that the level of civility in common daily encounters is considerably higher in Texas than elsewhere in America. When folks speak to you in a public place, they don't usually want your body, your money, or your time. As a rule, they're just being friendly. There's a lot of "ma'am-ing" and "suh-ing" that goes on. "Hidy" is the universal conversation opener, whether you've just been stopped for speeding by the Highway Patrol or you're approached by a lady of the night.

We Texans are a sadly chauvinistic lot, with a highly developed sense of state identity. When wandering around the continent most of us call "Yurip," Texans will, if asked where they are from, generally reply, "Texas," rather than, "The United States." Some of this chauvinism stems from our history. We were an independent nation before joining the United States—and sometimes act as though we still are. Some of it comes from the vagaries our school system; we study as much Texas history as we do American history. If visitors will kindly bear in mind that provincialism is a universal characteristic, our bragging will be easier to take.

Texas is mostly too hot. I recommend spring (which comes early) and fall (which starts late) as the best times to travel the state. In winter, anywhere south of Austin is apt to be fine, but if you come in the summer, well, it's just hot, that's all. No matter what time of year you come, there'll be some kind of civic whoopee and fandangle going on—the Cuero Turkey Trot, the Luling Watermelon Thump, or the Houston Fat Stock Show. Just about every city and town in Texas has its own annual hoorah. In Pharr, they celebrate onions, and in Athens, it's black-eyed peas. And there are rodeos and county fairs year-round. The friendly folks at the Texas Tourist Development Agency can provide you with a list of all these municipal kickups.

"To a Texan, a car is like wings to a seagull," Ronnie Dugger once wrote. "Our places are far apart and we must dip into them driving." There are a few good train trips in the state, and if you are interested only in cities, you can do it by plane, but this is a place best traveled by car. The great slabs of freeways will get you from one city to another in jig time, but the better way, I think, is to wander the primary highways, the better to see the landscapes and visit the towns.

Texas music includes mariachis, blues, country, and soul. Texas has produced two significant variations on country music. The first was country swing, a cross between country and the big-band sound, invented by the late Bob Wills. The second innovation was progressive country, a country style more sophisticated in both music and lyrics than Nashville country music. All over Texas, music is best enjoyed in your basic honkytonk. Every town has a few of 'em, down-home nightclubs. The dress is boots, jeans, and cowboy hats. Texans like to dance—either the two-step or a kind of country-music jitterbug. You can pick up the steps to the Cotton-eyed Joe, where folks dance four or eight to a line with their arms slung across each other's shoulders, in any honkytonk.

Some of the best-known honkytonks are Billy Bob's Texas in Fort Worth, Gilley's in the Houston suburb of Pasadena, the Cotton Club in Lubbock, and Rio Palm Isles in Longview. Tejanos (Texas Chicanos) are producing an amazing amount of good new music these days in styles called Tex-Mex, *norteño, ranchero,* and *conjunto.* The best-known Tejano band is Little Joe, Johnny y La Familia. They play in halls across Texas, and should you run across them, don't miss the performance. In most big Texas cities you can find good black or R & B clubs.

Perhaps the prettiest part of the state is the Hill Country of Central Texas. The Balcones Fault marks the line where the plains crumple up into the hills and the start of limestone country with its springs, rivers, and lakes. San Antonio remains the Hispanic capital of Texas and is crammed with history and fine attractions like the lovely riverwalk Paseo del Rio. I'm afraid it's impossible for me to debunk the Alamo: We may have lost, but we put up one hell of a good fight there, really an all-timer, like Thermopylae or Carthage. Besides which, we got so mad about losing that we went and stomped the Mexicans at the Battle of San Jacinto while yelling, "Remember the Alamo!" and we have been bragging about it ever since.

Austin, the state capital, is a mellow place noted for its innovative country music. It's the home of the university and the legislature, the finest free entertainment in Texas. The Lege meets for the first four months of odd-numbered years and during unpredictable special sessions after that. It beats the zoo or the circus, so catch it if it's in town. Austin's Sixth Street has become the Bourbon Street of Texas, and there's good live music all over town.

El Paso and its sister city of Ciudad Juárez have a flavor all their own. Both cities are markedly Mexican in feel, and the best restaurants serve real Mexican food, not Tex-Mex. Juárez nightlife ranges from chi-chi clubs to funky bars.

The two great cities of Texas are Houston and Dallas, both of which have almost as many detractors as avid fans. Houston has been described as "Los Angeles with the climate of Calcutta," and indeed the weather is so thoroughly miserable (hot and humid except for a few days a year when it's cold and humid) that before air conditioning took over, foreign diplomats used to get hardship pay for being posted there. Visitors will find that Houston has a compensating vitality and optimism about it that like to bowl you over. The sheer, raw energy of the place is astounding; it runneth over in all directions, sprawling across the Gulf coastal plain with complete abandon.

Dallas is considered Texas' "Eastern" city, by reputation a formal, proper, dressy place, self-consciously "cultural." It's a clean, well-lighted city, and compared to Houston it's almost fussy in its orderliness. A businessman's town, Dallas was built on the paper industries of insurance and banking. Its downtown is deader'n a doornail at night, but there's a cheerful night life in the Oak Lawn area and along Greenville Avenue. Neiman-Marcus remains one of the great class acts in the world of retail merchandising, and the lively apparel business in Dallas probably accounts for the city's "dressiness."

Fort Worth is the "cowtown" across the Trinity River that Dallas likes to look down on. It has a spunky, unpretentious charm of its own, and its old stockyard area is worth a visit.

THE HISTORY OF TEXAS

by
CONNIE SHERLEY

Connie Sherley has lived within a 35-mile radius of Austin her entire life. Before becoming a freelance travel writer—she is a member of the Society of American Travel Writers—Mrs. Sherley was travel editor of the Fentress Group Newspapers in Texas.

When Columbus discovered America, Texas was inhabited by several Indian tribes on a permanent basis, and some others as they felt the need to roam. The Caddoes were primarily farmers who got along with one another and stayed put. Hunting was good in the dense forests of North and East Texas where they lived, worked the land, and kept to themselves.

The Lipan Apaches covered the territory from San Antonio up into West Texas in a nomadic manner, leaving the coast to small tribes of less-tranquil Indians, the most notorious of whom were the Karankawas. After the first guidebook to Texas, Cabeza de Vaca's *Relación,* pointed out that the Karankawas were cannibalistic in addition to being mean *hombres,* knowledge of their presence discouraged casual landings along the Gulf of Mexico.

THE HISTORY OF TEXAS

The first notice of Texas by Europeans came in 1519, when Alonso Álvarez de Pineda mapped the Gulf coast from Florida to Vera Cruz, Mexico. He did no exploring; that came nine years later, when remnants of an ill-fated Spanish expedition washed up on the coast near Galveston. Led by Cabeza de Vaca, three survivors finally escaped from the Karankawas and made their way across Texas and down to Mexico City in 1536.

Cabeza de Vaca faded from New World history, but the seeds of greed he had sown with the tales of golden cities took root. The most famous search for the Seven Cities of Cibola was made by Francisco Vásquez de Coronado, who marched into Texas with three hundred well-armed conquistadores in 1540 and spent two years in the plains region, wandering as far as the Grand Canyon of the Colorado. The expedition failed to find cities of gold, but they left behind a boon to the Indians by releasing horses, which were to make the nomadic Indians more mobile.

The First Flag

The Spanish flag, first of six to fly over the state, was now firmly planted in Texas soil, but the new rulers made no attempt to colonize until the French fleur-de-lis flag was brought to the area in 1685 by Robert Cavelier Sieur de La Salle, an explorer with a splendid name but little sense of direction or luck. He and his men were looking for the mouth of the Mississippi but ended up at Lavaca Bay instead. He established Fort Saint Louis and began a search for silver and gold but then was killed by one of his own men. Disease and Indian raids eventually wiped out the fort, eliminating the French flag.

Actually, it took nearly two years for news of the French invasion to reach Mexico City and be relayed to Spain, where the absentee rulers decided that time had come for positive action. The first step was to give the territory a name. In 1689 Damian Massanet reported meeting Indians who proclaimed themselve *thecas,* or friends. There was debate about whether the word was *tejas, tayshas, texias* or *texas,* but the latter finally was accepted. In 1691 Texas-Coahuila was declared a dominion of Spain. Missions were established to Christianize the Indians, which was no small task, considering their nomadic nature. Initial attempts were made in East Texas, where the Caddos' stay-at-home ways created a better climate for conversion. The missionaries had some success, but it was the introduction of pigs, horses and cattle, farm implements, and European know-how, rather than religion, that laid a foundation for a culture destined to attract settlers.

A milestone in Texas history was the establishment of San Antonio de Valero mission and San Antonio de Alamo presidio, a garrison supplying military support, in 1718, as an outpost for the Mexican viceroy. Four more missions, San José, Concepción, San Juan

Capistrano, and Espada, followed on the banks of the San Antonio River.

Canary Islanders became the first of many outside ethnic groups to settle in Texas, when fifteen families were brought over in 1731 and given land at San Antonio. During the 1750s towns were formed on the Rio Grande, and in 1779 Nacogdoches was permanently established. Spanish paranoia about possible United States designs on the territory was fanned by the 1803 Louisiana Purchase and the Aaron Burr conspiracy, but problems were growing in Mexico. After Father Hidalgo led an unsuccessful revolt there in 1810 and 1811, Spain virtually ignored Texas.

The Old Three Hundred

Just before the Spanish period ended with Mexican independence in 1821, Moses Austin came to San Antonio from Missouri and applied for a colonization permit. The request was approved, but Austin died before he could make the next move. His son, Stephen F. Austin, a New Orleans attorney, took up the quest, obtaining permission to settle three hundred families. The Texas pilgrims, now called the Old Three Hundred, arrived by wagon train. Within a decade the original families had been joined by seven hundred more, and the colony at San Felipe had a population of five thousand.

Continuation of the empresario system begun by the Spanish encouraged colonization through land agents who received large grants for themselves and cheap land for settlers who accompanied them. Between 1821 and 1836 the population of Texas jumped from seven thousand to nearly fifty thousand as empresarios from both the United States and Mexico took advantage of the rulings.

Among the new arrivals was a Virginian named Sam Houston, who had grown up in Tennessee among the Indians and had developed an understanding of their ways that led to his distinguished service as a scout during the Indian wars. He subsequently became a lawyer, served in congress, and was governor of Tennessee when his bride, the daughter of one of the state's most influential and wealthy men, left him after their honeymoon. The scandal caused Houston to resign the governorship and head down the Texas Road to the Oklahoma Territory, where he stayed among his old boyhood friends, the Cherokees. Three years later, President Andrew Jackson asked Houston to go to Texas on a mission. Leaving his Indian wife, Tiana Rogers, behind, Houston went to San Antonio and later decided to settle in Nacogdoches.

Distance, language, and other cultural differences were rapidly corroding relations between Mexico and the Texas colonists. The Mexicans couldn't understand the Anglos' regard for law in the abstract or their dissatisfaction with a new constitution that failed to provide trial by jury and the right to bail. Neither could the Mexicans comprehend why the predominantly Protestant settlers were upset about a "paper law" requiring them to become Catholic. Sensing that the situation was getting out of control, the Mexican government decided in 1830 to cut off further settlement and imports from the United States.

In an attempt to work out some of the problems, Stephen F. Austin went to Mexico City and was promptly put in prison there. The experience convinced him that independence was the only answer.

The Alamo

Skirmishes between the colonists—now called Texians—and Mexican soldiers soon erupted into battles. On Oct. 2, 1835, Gonzales became the Lexington of Texas, but the Mexican president, Santa Anna, didn't become especially concerned about the rebels until they captured San Antonio on December 9, 1835. The defeat made Santa Anna angry enough to take command of the army and begin a march to San Antonio. By the time he arrived, the Texas force there had dwindled to fewer than two hundred men.

The Texians' commanders, Lieutenant Colonel William Barrett Travis and Colonel James Bowie, ordered their men into the walled chapel called the Alamo, hoping reinforcements would arrive before their situation became hopeless. Bowie was seriously ill with typhoid-pneumonia and had to be taken in on his cot. The seige began on February 24, the day after Santa Anna arrived with the first wave of his troops. The Mexican commander's daily demand for surrender was answered each time with a cannon shot.

Travis's appeals for help brought 32 men from Gonzales, who made their way through Mexican lines and entered the Alamo on March 1. Their arrival raised the Texians' ranks to 187 men. Three days later the remainder of Santa Anna's troops marched into San Antonio, which was now surrounded by 5,000 men.

On March 6, 1836, Santa Anna hoisted the red flag of no quarter on the San Fernando church tower. Just before dawn, with bugles sounding the *Deguello* ("Death to the Defenders"), columns of Mexican soldiers attacked all four walls. Twice they were driven back, but the third attack on the north wall was successful. Travis died at his cannon, and Davy Crockett and his Tennessee Boys fell in hand-to-hand fighting in front of the doors into the chapel. Bowie emptied his pistols and utilized his famous Bowie knife before he was killed. The thirteen-day siege ended in a few hours. The Texas force had no survivors. Santa Anna ordered the defenders' bodies burned.

During the siege the constitutional convention was in session at Washington-on-the-Brazos. Former members of the United States Congress, constitutional-convention representatives from Alabama and Missouri, fifteen attorneys, and six doctors were among the forty-four men who signed the Texas Declaration of Independence on March 2, 1836. David G. Burnet was named provisional governor, and Sam Houston continued as commander in chief of the army.

Military disasters continued for the Texians. Three weeks after the fall of the Alamo, Santa Anna ordered the massacre of more than three hundred prisoners at Goliad, fanning to a roar the rebels' fire of rage and indignation.

Sam Houston took his time regrouping the Texian forces as Santa Anna marched south to a point on Buffalo Bayou near the present site of Houston. The ragtag Texas army stalking the Mexicans had no uniforms and little artillery. On April 21, surrounded by 1,600 men, Santa Anna felt confident enough to take his usual siesta. After the camp had settled down for naps, 783 Texians came charging across the terrain shouting, "Remember the Alamo!" and "Remember Goliad!"

The Battle of San Jacinto was over in eighteen minutes. The Mexicans counted 630 dead, 280 wounded, and 730 taken prisoner, including Santa Anna, who remained a captive for six months. Nine Texians were killed or mortally wounded and thirty others sustained less-serious wounds. A rifle ball shattered Houston's ankle.

The Republic of Texas

The Treaty of Velasco, signed May 14, 1836, sent Santa Anna back to Mexico City, where he promptly denounced the new republic, but the United States, France, Great Britain, Holland, France, and some German states recognized the country, providing Texas with powerful diplomatic friends who discouraged full-scale invasion by Mexico. Sam Houston was elected president and Mirabeau B. Lamar vice-president. The people also voted in favor of annexation by the United States, but the Missouri Compromise of 1820 precluded Texas' becoming a state, since most Texas landowners had slaves. In 1838 the annexation proposal was withdrawn and the government settled into the job of organizing the republic. The distinctive red, white, and blue flag with the lone five-pointed star was officially adopted.

The republic period was a collection of financial and strategic disasters. Ships of the Texas navy were repossessed when repair bills couldn't be paid. Mexico refused to recognize Texas' independence, which led the republic into skirmishes and foolhardy expeditions into Mexico and New Mexico that cost both lives and money.

The capital was moved from Washington-on-the-Brazos to Columbia to Houston. Finally Austin was selected as the permanent capital site during Lamar's presidency, much to Houston's displeasure. Austin citizens suspected that after his reelection, Houston might try to move the capital back to his namesake city, so they put a protective watch on the state archives.

During one of the periodic Mexican invasions, Houston did, indeed, send two Texas Rangers to move the archives to Washington-on-the-Brazos for "safekeeping." A woman caught the rangers loading the archives and sounded the alarm by firing a six-pound cannon kept loaded for the purpose. The rangers and the archives took off in a wagon, but the citizen recruits, dragging the cannon, caught them as they camped overnight and gave the rangers a choice of fighting or surrendering the archives. They selected surrender, ending the Archives War and returning the government records to Austin.

The only commodity the republic had was land. At this time the Texas Republic's boundary followed the Rio Grande to its source through New Mexico into what is today southern Colorado, where it took a stovepipe cut into Wyoming and included portions of Kansas and Oklahoma. The General Land Office was established to handle this huge public domain. The empresario system was continued, further spurring settlement, which in turn stirred up the Indians.

The prospect of cheap land in a climate of personal choice and freedom attracted settlers from the southern United States, where slavery was increasingly becoming a heated issue. Several hundred Germans, including noblemen who hoped to make a profit as empresarios, formed the Verein zum Schutze Deutscher Einwanderer, which sponsored 7,380 German colonists from 1844 to 1846, when the Verein went bankrupt. A second group, Irish settlers, arrived in 1848, and Czechoslovakian families, eager to escape the wars that regularly overran their homeland, began to immigrate in large numbers. Poles, Swedes, Danes, and Wends arrived in Galveston and pushed inland, bringing their religions, skills, and cultures to a new setting. In all, twenty-six ethnic groups formed the nucleus of early Texas settlement.

Statehood

Eventually, it was Great Britain's interest in Texas that led to statehood. The British had no intention of adding the republic to their empire, but they felt that an independent Texas would be a deterrent to the United States' western expansion, since Texas' far-flung borders would create a barrier. Trade with Texas offered Britain commercial advantages, as well as an opportunity to muddy American economic and social affairs.

After the United States senate again rejected annexation in 1844, the question became an issue in the presidential campaign. When James Polk, who favored annexation, defeated Henry Clay, President John Tyler carried out the electorate's wishes by pushing Texas statehood through congress as one of his last acts of office.

With prodding from Great Britain, Mexico offered to recognize Texas' independence if statehood was refused, but sentiment in Texas was for annexation. Sentiment aside, the Texas public debt had risen to nearly eight million dollars, and the support of United States revenues was welcome. An annexation ordinance was adopted in Texas July 4, 1845. The following October the people approved a state constitution in which Texas reserved ownership of its public lands and retained the right to divide into five separate states—a plan that has been proposed at least sixteen times but never approved. The United States congress accepted the Texas constitution December 29, 1845, making Texas the twenty-eighth state in the union.

The Lone Star flag was lowered from the capitol in Austin February 19, 1846, and the Stars and Stripes became the fifth flag to fly over Texas. Texians became Texans when they became Americans, for a reason shrouded by history but probably having something to do with logical spelling.

Almost immediately Mexico launched an attack, and the United States retaliated. The Mexican War ended February 2, 1848, with the Treaty of Hidalgo.

Then Texas got into a boundary dispute with the United States, after which the Compromise of 1850 brought Texas ten million dollars in exchange for claims to land on either side of the Rio Grande. The windfall allowed the state to pay its debts and set two million dollars aside for a permanent school fund that, in 1854, led to a statewide network of free public schools.

Sam Houston returned to the political arena, serving as a United States senator for two terms before successfully running for Texas governor in 1859. Because of the vast distances within the state, and to get goods to distant markets, Texas was eager to have railroads. An offer of five sections of land (3,200 acres) for each mile of track was made to the companies. When there were no takers, the land grant was raised to sixteen sections. The plan eventually gave the railroads more than thirty-two million acres, mostly in West Texas, where it was subsequently sold to settlers for $1.50 an acre.

Hostile Indians and lack of water slowed West Texas development, but one of those problems was eliminated in 1854 by the first American windmill. The railroads brought the invention to Texas, primarily to supply water for steam engines, but its use quickly spread, making the vast dry areas of the Panhandle and West Texas inhabitable.

Texas in the Confederacy

Before the economic benefits that would result from railroads and the windmill could be felt, the issue of secession, in the dispute over slavery, became paramount. Houston, now governor, opposed secession, but the people were predominantly southerners. As states' righters, they opposed a strong federal government even if they weren't pro-slavery. Texas seceded from the Union January 28, 1861, and the Confederate flag replaced the Stars and Stripes to become the sixth flag. When Houston refused to take an oath of allegiance to the Confederacy, the Secession Convention removed him from office.

The Texas coast was blockaded during the Civil War, and the state's prime port, Galveston, was captured by the United States and then recaptured by the Confederates. For the most part there was little fighting on Texas soil; however, the war's last land battle took place deep in the Rio Grande Valley near Brownsville, an area so remote that a Confederate force captured eight hundred federal soldiers May 13, 1865, only to have their startled prisoners tell them that Lee had surrendered at Appomattox more than a month earlier.

Reconstruction was a bitter period. The predominantly rural population was busy trying to revitalize farms and ranches neglected during the war. Cattle provided the only bright economic note. The hardy longhorn had multiplied at a tremendous rate on the open range. The problem was getting them to markets hundreds of miles away. Fortunately, the longhorn is a fine traveler. Herds of twenty-five hundred to three thousand were moved north along the famous cattle trails—Chisholm, Western-Dodge, and Shawnee—to slaughter pens as far away as the Canadian border.

Cattle raising was a hard life that created cattle kingdoms and spawned the cowboy, who learned professional rudiments from the *vaqueros* and also borrowed the Mexican cowboy's trappings: leather chaps, bandannas, spurs, the lariat, boots, and a broadbrimmed hat capable of warding off the weather, be it rain or the fierce Texas sun.

Range Wars and Railroads

It was 1879 before barbed wire was sold in quantity, but John "Bet a Million" Gates soon became its leading salesman and set up manufacturing companies to meet demand. Enclosing the open ranges set off feuds between cattlemen and ranchers, and the feuds led to fence cutting. In 1884 a special session of the legislature was called to deal with the problem. As a result, fence cutting and malicious pasture burning became felony crimes in Texas. The fenced range brought a new era in cattle breeding, which had gotten off to a fancy start in 1848 when two cows and a bull from Queen Victoria's Durham herd were imported to a North Texas ranch.

The railroads were developing quickly. Dallas was served by one line, but word got out that the new Texas and Pacific Railroad had selected a site twenty miles away as the point where the new line and the existing railroad would intersect, creating an important cross site that would challenge Dallas in importance. When the legislature passed the Texas and Pacific charter, the charter contained a provision written in at the last minute by a Dallas legislator stipulating that the cross site must be "no more than a mile from Browder Springs." The bill became law before the legislators from the rest of the state discovered that Browder Springs was in effect part of Dallas, the source of Dallas' water supply, about a mile from the site of Neely's first cabin—the beginning of Dallas. The strategic rail position caused a growth flurry that raised Dallas' population from twelve hundred to seven thousand in a few months. The town quickly became a leading distribution point for the Southwest, attracting ambitious merchants and businessmen with a penchant for establishing banks and insurance companies.

After the capitol burned in 1881, plans began for a new building on the grounds in Austin, although the state had no money. To finance the project, three million acres of Texas Panhandle land were offered in exchange for a building contract. An Illinois syndicate took up the offer and turned the land into the famous XIT Ranch.

The late nineteenth century was a period of slow development for Texas' agricultural economy, but important changes were taking place in other ways. Fifty miles inland, upstart Houston had dredged Buffalo Bayou into a channel capable of handling oceangoing ships. Houston's port status, combined with its excellent rail facilities, gained added importance in 1900 when Texas' more important port, Galveston, was hit by the worst natural disaster in American history—a hurricane that killed more than six thousand people and virtually closed Galveston.

Black Gold

Oil had been something of a nuisance in Texas for years. People dug for badly needed water, only to have the well ruined by seeping oil. The first producing well, drilled in 1866, was abandoned because there was no market for the product. In 1896, with a market for oil slowly developing, the Corsicana oil field led to the building of the state's first refinery.

Texas' big-time entry into the oil age came January 10, 1901, when Spindletop blew in near Beaumont. During the wild period that followed, hundreds of oil companies were formed. Some survived. The barbed-wire king, "Bet a Million" Gates, started the Texas Company, which would become Texaco. Gulf and Humble also began with Spindletop leases. Black gold would upstage cotton, wheat, and cattle in the state's economic picture.

The flat land around Houston was perfect for pipelines, and the ship channel made an ideal refinery site. Best of all, Houston bankers were willing to take chances on exploration financing. The new port city was a natural headquarters for the fledgling oil industry.

In Dallas on September 10, 1907, oil money got a new market when Neiman-Marcus opened for business. Political destiny entered the world with the birth of Lyndon Baines Johnson, August 28, 1908.

More rich oil fields were discovered throughout East and West Texas. (In 1923 the University of Texas became one of the richest schools in the country when Santa Rita Number 1 came in on land set aside for the university during republic days.)

The state's mild winters and dry climate made it a military headquarters during World War I. The forerunner of the Army Air Force was founded at Fort Sam Houston in San Antonio in 1910 and expanded to Kelly Field during World War I. Originally all pilot training took place outside the Alamo City at Randolph Air Field, the "West Point of the Air."

Texas became the first state to elect a woman governor in 1924, when Miriam "Ma" Ferguson ran for the office because a prior impeachment made her husband ineligible. She lost a bid for a second term but made a successful comeback six years later and served two more years.

Water had always been one of the state's biggest problems. There was either too little or too much. Heavy rains set the rivers on rampages that caused loss of property and life. Droughts wiped out farms and ranches. In the late 1930s, construction began on a series of dams that would tame the rivers and provide new sources of irrigation and power, as well as a mammoth watery patchwork of recreational lakes.

World War II and After

When the United States moved into the defense period that preceded World War II, Texas' low tax rate, excellent climate, and good labor market brought an influx of industry. Government aircraft plants were built in the Dallas–Fort Worth area, and additional army, air force, and naval training bases were opened in Texas.

Lyndon Johnson was elected to the United States Senate in 1947 by a margin of eighty-seven votes that earned him the nickname "Landslide Lyndon." Within four years he was the senate majority whip, and, with Sam Rayburn of Texas serving as Speaker of the House, Texas had unprecedented influence in Washington. By 1950 Texas businessmen were wooing large companies and industries to relocate in the state, and the industrial migration was in full swing. For the first time in the state's history, the census showed more Texans living in cities than in rural areas.

By now irrigation had become the greatest thing for Texas farmers and ranchers since the windmill. Sophisticated networks of manmade rainfall turned the high plains into one of the nation's prime wheat-, grain-, and cotton-growing areas. The oil industry evolved to the petrochemical industry centered on the Gulf coast.

Since the Aerospace Medical Center and the Air Force's Air Training Command headquarters were in Texas, it seemed logical that the Manned Space Center (MSC) should be built on a thousand acres of former swampland outside Houston donated to the government by Rice University. Naturally, there were those who felt Vice-President Johnson's role as chairman of the National Aeronautics and Space Council had as much to do with the decision as the free land, but be that as it may, the MSC put Texas up front in the space age.

Nov. 22, 1963, John F. Kennedy was assassinated in Dallas and Lyndon Johnson became president of the United States.

By the 1970s Texas was the world's most air-conditioned area, and its citizens were noted for dashing from air-conditioned homes to air-conditioned cars to air-conditioned offices and shopping malls. Surrounded as they were by oil and its byproducts, the world petroleum crisis took on an ironic aspect for Texans waiting in gas-station lines.

The increase in oil prices turned the Texas weather into a valuable natural resource and made the state the most attractive notch in the much-publicized Sun Belt. Space-age industries followed the lead of electronics companies that had relocated in Texas during the 1950s and '60s. Population boomed, particularly in the Houston, Dallas, and San Antonio areas, putting the three among the eleven largest United States cities in the 1980 census.

TEXAS FOOD AND DRINK

by
CONNIE SHERLEY

Texans are born knowing the difference between chile, chili, and chile con carne. This intuitive hereditary touch complements the asbestos palates with which we also are said to come into this world.

Consider that chile is to chili is to chile con carne, a formula outsiders find more difficult to comprehend than the theory of relativity, which is precisely what it is; but instead of being relative to the universe, this matter is relative to Tex-Mex, the state's own cuisine. Without chiles there would be no chili, and without chili there would be no Tex-Mex.

Chiles are peppers that grow in a variety of sizes packed with a wide range of sizzle. Chili is the traditional "bowl of red," produced by slowly cooking chopped beef, chiles, and the chef's own blend of spices, which always includes cumin, a special ingredient brought to Texas in 1731 by Canary Islanders who settled in San Antonio. True Texas chili is never cooked with beans. The subject is undebatable.

Since *chile con carne* translates to "peppers with meat," chili con carne (if such a thing existed) would be a meat dish with meat, a redundancy on a par with "Rio Grande River"—which, incidentally, is where it all began when Mexican chiles were brought north and combined with slow cooking to make tough, stringy beef from the hardy Texas longhorn palatable.

Like most things Texan, the origination of chili is steeped in legend made more colorful with each passing decade. Many historians—and the state abounds with experts on the subject—claim that chili was created in the San Antonio jail during Texas Republic days when an imaginative cook chopped up meat of questionable vintage before simmering it with chiles and anything else he thought might mask the taint. The dish got better with each reheating, and prisoners supposedly developed such a passion for the pungent mixture that they refused freedom when their sentences were completed.

The story is certainly plausible, for the addiction has been handed down as part of the Lone Star heritage. When the first norther puts a nip of fall in the air, twentieth-century Texans are overcome by a craving that can be sated only by a steaming bowl of chili and a stack of crisp saltine crackers, which are lovingly crumbled into the bowl of red. (Dipping saltines into the dish is a *faux pas* of the highest magnitude.)

West Texans attribute the origination of chili to chuck-wagon cooks called upon to satisfy the palates of cowboys who snacked on pequins, small wild chiles considered the most potent of peppers.

If time hadn't wiped out, or at least blurred, the tracks of truth on the subject, credit probably would go to a combination of sources that merged in San Antonio, where *lavanderas* began a moonlighting operation to augment their incomes as laundresses and developed the first fast-food operation, ladling chili from wash pots set up around the plazas. Nineteenth-century writers vividly describe the chili queens' stands ringing the squares and the mouthwatering, spicy scents that drew customers into the area.

The era ended in 1937, when modern health ordinances forced the chili queens out of business. By then their menus had been expanded to include tortillas and tamales served on long portable tables made of sawhorses and boards. The outdoor enterprises were the forerunners of Tex-Mex restaurants.

Tex-Mex

During the chili-queen period, almost every Texas town was fortunate enough to have a man of Mexican heritage who mounted a big tin can filled with steaming tamales packaged in corn shucks on a pushcart and set up shop along Main Street. As financial pressures of the Depression began to ease, tamale salesmen sensed their clientele's desire for expanded services, as well as an opportunity to get in out of the fickle Texas weather, and opened restaurants in their homes. The three-generation businesses utilized Grandmother's talents in the kitchen, Mama's and Papa's supervision in the dining room, and the children's energy taking care of the tables.

As word of mouth spread, additional rooms furnished with second-hand tables and chrome chairs were opened. The less atmosphere a place had, it seemed, the better the food was. South-of-the-border recipes were adapted to north-of-the-border tastes, but chili gravy, which is chili with a minimum of meat, was the cohesive ingredient. The menu was based on the regular plate: an enchilada, rice, refried beans, and a tamale, which evolved to the special plate with the optional addition of either a taco or *chile con queso.*

For the uninitiated, an enchilada might best be described as a Mexican crepe. It begins with a tortilla made of masa, a special corn flour, combined with exactly the right amount of water. The dough is patted out to a flat pancake and baked on a grill. Some cooks heat the tortilla in chili gravy; others douse it in hot lard before rolling the softened tortilla around grated longhorn or Monterey Jack cheese and chopped onion. The rolls are covered with more chili gravy, sprinkled with additional grated cheese and onion, and heated until the cheese melts and the sauce bubbles.

The first Tex-Mex restaurants heated and served the food on the same heavy brown pottery plates. The feast was always presented with the admonition, "Hot plate—very hot plate."

After World War II the taco took on added dimension and crumbling power when an Austin restaurant, El Matamoros, began serving a tortilla that erupted with thin bubbles when deep fried. The crisp, puffy product exploded into tiny pieces if touched by a fork, a misfortune that befell only outsiders bent on adhering to Emily Post's rules. Texans know that tacos, like fried chicken, were meant to be eaten by hand.

The innovation made Austin the state's acknowledged Tex-Mex cuisine capital. Around the state, restaurants advertised, "We serve Austin-style Tex-Mex," which meant that a puffy tortilla would be wrapped round the seasoned ground meat garnished with chopped tomato and lettuce if you ordered a taco, and the same base would be used for *chile con queso,* a blending of at least two cheeses and chiles. The two dishes, combined with a serving of guacamole, make up the popular salad plate, guaranteed not to offend the most timid taste buds.

The original regular plate has evolved to include a variety of combinations through the years, as Tex-Mex has gradually embraced new dishes. Guacamole was a natural addition inhibited only by the availability of the avocado. The basic ingredient is mashed to a lumpy consistency, perked up with seasonings, and combined with finely chopped tomato.

Chile rellenos slipped into Texas from New Mexico, and were allowed to stay because the bland chiles, stuffed with a variety of fillings before being batter fried, are such a delicious addition. The same goes for fajitas, skirt steaks the Mexicans turn into a delicacy by marinating them and quick grilling them over charcoal. The meat slices are served in flour tortillas, refined cousins of the masa variety. Carne asada is similar, but the chunks of beef are usually garnished with pico de gallo, a sauce of tomatoes, chiles, onion, chopped avocado, and cilantro leaves.

Which brings us to sauces. The quality of the *salsa picante* can make or break a restaurant. The basic condiment is freshly made of chiles, tomatoes, onion, garlic, and cilantro, finely chopped. It is a dip for tostados, the quartered, crisply fried tortillas served in baskets, and provides added zip when Texans want more fire in a dish. It should be capable of clearing the sinuses when the dosage is doubled. Beware of seeds in salsa. They carry capsaicin, the chiles' punch.

Of the seemingly endless array of new dishes on Tex-Mex menus, only the nacho was conceived north of the border. June 1, 1971, was a date that changed the Texas restaurant scene. Among other things, the arrival of liquor by the drink through a change in state law created a need for an appetizer on Tex-Mex menus. Who can sip margaritas without nibbling? Tortillas were quartered, fried to a crisp, topped with refried beans and cheese, popped into the oven until the cheese melted, and then crowned with a sliver of jalapeño (hal-uh-*pain*-nyuh). The nacho is the supreme Tex-Mex hors d'oeuvre.

The Margarita

The margarita was on the south bank of the Rio Grande, just waiting for Texas to shake off its archaic liquor laws. One part each of pure lime juice (connoisseurs use only the Mexican variety) and triple sec or Cointreau, and two parts tequila are either given a good tumbling with crushed ice in a cocktail shaker and strained or served on the rocks after being blended sans ice. The glass rim is doused with lime juice and dipped in coarse salt, so the margarita can be sipped through the coating. Definitely not for those on a low-sodium diet.

Just as Tex-Mex is blasphemed through fast-food sour-cream "tacos" garnished with ripe olives, the margarita has been desecrated with a frozen version of the drink that amounts to a tequila-touched snowcone piled into fancy glasses. Powders and bottled "reconstituted" lime juice, touted as substitutes for fresh lime juice, have found their way into bars, but just as sure as chiles make chili, there is no shortcut to a fine margarita.

On the changing Tex-Mex scene, two things remain constant. The first is the last: the dessert course. Forget the pastry cart and other devious offerings meant only to appeal to the sweet tooth, pad the tab, pour on calories, and/or make you forget how lousy the entree was. Tex-Mex needs only a pecan praline or lime or pineapple sherbet.

The Lone Star praline bears no resemblance to European confections of the same name. Texas pralines are made by cooking sugar and cream or buttermilk to a golden brown. The syrup is beaten until creamy, laced with pecans, and dropped by spoonfuls to harden into patties. Pralines stretched with coconut merit the same disdain as frozen margaritas.

Texans are about equally divided between pralines and sherbet as the perfect ending to the meal; however, the sherbet isn't meant to be a palate-clearing sorbet. The idea is moot because of Tex-Mex's natural lingering qualities.

Tex-Mex Champagne: Beer

Beer, the other constant on the Tex-Mex scene, has been legal in Texas since the repeal of Prohibition, so there has never been any problem concerning what to drink with a Tex-Mex meal. Wine does nothing for the cuisine, but cold beer, served in an icy mug, complements each bite. Beer drinkers are loyal to Lone Star, Pearl, and Shiner, the last of which remains the principal product of the South Texas town (population 2,213) bearing the same name.

Where else but in Texas will you find a beer garden on the National Register of Historic Places? Scholz Garten, on the fringe of the University of Texas in Austin, has been pouring suds since 1866. Customers order by the pitcher or in the Lone Star trademark, the long-neck bottle. German immigrants endowed the state with a beer culture that continued without interruption through Prohibition, with homebrew produced in cellars and smokehouses.

Texas Barbecue

Beer also lends itself nicely to barbecue, the second most renowned eating habit in the state. The predecessor of modern barb-q began in ranch pits where whole steers were cooked over wood coals. Texas barbecue got international attention, or notoriety, when Lyndon Johnson had the barbecue master Walter Jetton cater gatherings in Washington and at the Texas White House.

The statewide popularity of barbecue goes back to the time when Saturday was set aside for weekly shopping. Farmers brought their families to town and spent the day gathering supplies. The rural folk were skeptical of what few restaurants existed, and boardinghouses were always crowded already. To feed the crowds, meat-market owners built pits in back of their shops and started slow cooking brisket, ribs, and rings of sausage, known as hot links. The patient process began on Friday night. By Saturday morning the air floated with the delicious smoky aroma, whetting the appetites of townspeople, who quickly joined the Saturday barbecue tradition. Meats, sold by the pound, were eaten picnic-style off heavy, rosy-pink butcher paper.

The best barbecue is found in unpretentious small-town establishments with interiors permeated by the essence of smoked meats. Anyone who thinks all barbecue is dry and tough should drop by Joe Cotton's in Robstown, Louie Mueller's in Taylor, or the Kruez Market in Lockhart.

Add cole slaw, potato salad, sliced onions, dill pickles, jalapeño peppers, sliced white bread, iced tea, and kegs of Lone Star, Pearl, or Shiner beer to barbecue, and you have an occasion that has won votes for many politicians and marked holidays, weddings, anniversaries, and birthdays in Texas for several generations.

Other Texas Favorites

Oh, yes, "ahst" tea, another Lone Star phenomenon. Failure to specify hot tea when ordering in Texas will get you a tall glass of iced tea, regardless of the time of day. Texans drink vast amounts of iced tea morning, noon, and night. Nothing takes the sting out of a hot summer day like a big, thirst-quenching glass of orange pekoe over ice.

The native soft drink is Dr. Pepper, prepared from a formula worked out by a Waco druggist who wanted something different to bring customers to his soda fountain. For years Dr. Pepper, like Fritos, was marketed only within the state. Traveling Texans who carried private stocks of the soft drink and the crunchy snack based on corn tortillas are credited with creating a demand for the products all over the world.

One of the joys of driving through Texas is the opportunity it provides for sampling local specialties: homemade breads from the bakeries at Fredericksburg; wursts from the meat markets of New Braunfels; and kolaches, the fruit- or cheese-filled Czechoslovakian pastries from West. Be alert for festivals and fairs where local cooks strive to excel by producing ethnic dishes seldom seen other places.

Texas home cooking was heavily influenced by Southerners who brought along a love for fried chicken, hot biscuits, and rich sweet desserts when they migrated to Texas. Because corn was more plentiful than wheat, cornbread became the staff of life. Today nutritionists have declared beans and cornbread, the pioneers' staple, to be one of the best-balanced, most protein-rich dishes.

In a spirit of making do, cooks substituted peaches for apples and pecans for walnuts in recipes. And somewhere along the line beef was given the batter treatment, and the infamous Texas chicken-fried steak came into being. This entrée is the mainstay on menus of small-town cafés and city restaurants catering to rural expatriates. Non-Texans have been known to describe chicken-fried steaks and the mandatory cream gravy that accompanies them to a shoe sole coated with batter, fried, and slathered with well-peppered Elmer's glue. Texans excuse the comparison as ignorance of the better things in life. They remember that it has taken the rest of the country a long time to get tuned in to the culinary joys of fried okra and good-luck-producing quantities of black-eyed peas eaten on New Year's Day—joys long recognized in Texas.

The need to disguise Texas beef evaporated years ago. Some of the most flavorful and tender steaks available are served at restaurants like Cattlemen's in Fort Worth and the Night Hawk in Austin. There's no charge for the 72-ounce sirloin at the Big Texan in Amarillo, provided you clean your plate within an hour. Yes, it's even possible to get a steak cooked rare, a bit of progress few Texans would have bet on a decade ago.

You must be wondering if a visit to Texas is going to limit you to provincial eating. Remember the statement that June 1, 1971, changed the Texas restaurant scene? The new liquor laws did more than end brown bagging and legalize margaritas. As wines began to flow freely in the state, the need arose for foods beyond Tex-Mex, barbecue, and steaks, all of which lend themselves best just to beer and iced tea.

Young Texans who had developed a liking for foreign cuisines while traveling abroad opened trendy cafés to showcase their newly acquired cooking abilities. The opportunity for a profit margin from the sale of cocktails and wines encouraged excellent chefs who'd been imported to the state by hotels to leave the corporate kitchens and start their own restaurants.

New arrivals from the Far East, lured by wide-open spaces in the Sun Belt and the Lone Star mystique, have introduced Indian, Szechuan, Thai, and Vietnamese dishes that sound foreign but taste familiar because of that common denominator, the chile. Their family-owned and -operated restaurants are reminiscent of the first Tex-Mex places that made eating out so much fun.

Chefs specializing in nouvelle cuisine and Continental cooking are making the most of the excellent fresh shrimp, crab, red snapper, and flounder brought in from the Gulf of Mexico. In the past five years, some of the country's finest restaurants have emerged in Texas cities. The reputation of several Dallas haute cuisine establishments is so widespread that reservations were booked two years in advance by delegates to the 1984 Republican convention.

Texans have always believed the best is none too good, which is why they point with pride to places like Jefferson, the East Texas hamlet with a firm hold on the past. Few meals served anywhere compare to the tradition and excellence of the plantation breakfast at Jefferson's Excelsior House: grits, cured ham, scrambled eggs, and the lightest biscuits and orange muffins you'll ever put into your mouth.

There have been many changes since the late Helen Corbitt introduced a new level of eating excellence in the Zodiac Room at

Neiman-Marcus, but one thing remains constant: The sure way to start a debate is to walk up to a group of Texans and ask directions to the best Tex-Mex restaurant in town. Eight people will come up with at least five different answers—and they'll all be right.

DALLAS AND FORT WORTH

The Metroplex

**by
KAREN ARRINGTON JORDAN**

Karen Arrington Jordan, a member of the Society of American Travel Writers, is Travel Editor of the Dallas Morning News, *having previously been an assistant travel editor for the paper, an editor with the* Abilene (Texas) Reporter-News, *and an editorial intern with the Southwest Bureau (Dallas) of the* Wall Street Journal. *A native of the Texas Gulf coast, she is an alumna of Texas A & M University (College Station).*

Parts of the Practical Information section were produced by Elizabeth Logan, dining critic of the Dallas Morning News *and a frequent contributor to* D (Dallas) *magazine and* Houston City *magazine.*

If you've heard of Dallas—and TV producers are certain you have—you've also heard it is "a city that never should have been." There is no major waterway (Dallas's version of the Trinity River is little more than a nuisance), and there are few resources. Dallasites—more than a few, incidentally, chuckle that the TV show "never should have been"—have made the city what it is today, the nation's 7th largest (a few shy of 1 million) and a center of commerce, banking, insurance, and transportation.

For "a city that never should have been" there certainly are car- and planeloads of people who want to come to the Metroplex, a metropolitan statistical area including also Fort Worth, the Mid-Cities, and encircling towns, and suburbs, with a total population of 3.1 million—a 25 percent increase over 10 years ago. These visitors want to play, and many want to stay. Now the country's third leading city in number of headquartered million-dollar companies and in concentration of corporate headquarters, Dallas is also among the nation's top five cities in convention activities, fashion markets, film, electronics, and insurance centers. It is also the largest cotton trading center in the nation, the largest wholesale merchandise mart in the world, and the largest gift and home furnishing market in the United States. Some 400 of the 500 largest industrial corporations listed in *Fortune* have representatives, divisions, subsidiaries, or affiliates in the Metroplex. And over 200 metroplex-based corporations are traded on the New York and the American Stock Exchanges and in the over-the-counter market.

Dallas works. It's more business than talk, not only from finance to fashion, but also from airport to architecture, from sports to churches. If not the most colorful city around, it certainly is clean and cultural.

The Southwest's banking center, Big D is home to 243 insurance companies; more than 125 firms serve the oil industry here. The world's fourth busiest airport, Dallas–Fort Worth, is bigger than the island of Manhattan and, naturally, is the country's largest landing strip. Any glossy photograph of the glassy Dallas skyline—and likewise of neighbor-to-the-west Fort Worth's—is out of date by the time it comes back from the developer. Any older buildings left standing—after wrecking crews clear a space for a new hotel, office, or apartment building—are being renovated.

The downtown's "signature" building is perhaps the 50-story Reunion Tower, adjacent to the Hyatt Regency at 300 Reunion Boulevard.

Vehicular traffic fades, for the most part, with the sun's setting on a hectic business day in both downtown Dallas and Fort Worth—the exceptions being nights of concerts and, in Dallas, professional basketball games. The pedestrian and the touring motorist have the areas to themselves; but for that reason—and as in most major cities—nighttime is not the wisest time for a visitor to take in the downtown landmarks of either city. Except for downtown hotels, most businesses are closed. However, John Neely Bryan's Cabin, John F. Kennedy Memorial Plaza, Dealey Plaza, and Union Station are all in the revitalized west end of Dallas's business district.

DALLAS AND FORT WORTH

Points of Interest

1) Adolphus Hotel
2) Concert Hall (Planned)
3) Convention and Visitors Bureau (in the Chamber of Commerce)
4) Dallas Centre Complex
5) Dallas Hilton
6) Dallas Memorial Auditorium and Convention Center
7) New Dallas Museum of Art (Arts District under dev.)
8) Farmer's Market
9) Greyhound/Trailways Terminal
10) Hyatt Regency Hotel
11) JFK Memorial Plaza
12) Majestic Theater
13) Municipal Building
14) Neiman-Marcus
15) New Arts Theater
16) Old City Park
17) Plaza of the Americas
18) Public Library
19) Reunion Tower
20) Texas School Book Depository
21) Thanksgiving Square
22) Union Station
23) Visitor Information Center

At day's end, Dallasites desert downtown, mostly for points north, especially to the restaurant and club scenes of Greenville Avenue, parallel to and just east of Central Expressway (U.S. 75)—the road to Richardson and Plano—and near Southern Methodist University (in Highland Park) and NorthPark Shopping Center; the Bachman Lake area of Northwest Highway, northwest of Love Field; and Addison, a Far North Dallas suburb bounded by popular Prestonwood Town Center shopping mall. If Dallas shoppers are not "charging it" at NorthPark or Prestonwood, chances are they've found a parking spot at the multilevel Galleria or nearby at Valley View Mall, both in an area between Dallas Parkway and Preston Road on LBJ Freeway (Loop 635), a fifteen-mile drive north via the Dallas North Tollway from downtown.

Points east of downtown Dallas lead to the Texas State Fair Grounds, which includes the Cotton Bowl and myriad museums, and on to Mesquite and northeast to Garland. White Rock Lake Park—a haunt of joggers, bicyclists, lakeside fishermen, sailors, and picnickers—lies to the northeast of downtown in the East Dallas–Casa Linda residential sections of town.

Equidistant from downtown on U.S. 35E are Marsalis Park and Zoo to the south in Oak Cliff and Dallas Market Center to the north-northwest. In the latter direction, Stemmons Freeway leads to Farmers Branch, Carrollton, and Lewisville, but football fans take the Texas 183 exit off north 35E west to suburban Irving, home of Texas Stadium. The south entrance to Dallas–Fort Worth Airport is "just down the road a piece"; the north entrance is accessible from both Texas 114 (the road to Grapevine) and the western extension of Loop 635.

A fifteen- to twenty-minute drive west of downtown Dallas—or east of downtown Cowtown (Fort Worth)—along I-30 (also known as the Old Dallas–Fort Worth Turnpike), the Metroplex's greatest concentration of theme and amusement parks is centered in Grand Prairie and Arlington: Six Flags Over Texas, Arlington Stadium (home of baseball's Texas Rangers), Wet 'n Wild, Southwest Historical Wax Museum, International Wildlife Park, and the Fire Museum of Texas.

Serious Sports

Sports are also big business in Dallas–Fort Worth. The Dallas Cowboys of the National Football League play in the 65,000-seat Texas Stadium in Irving, the majority of which is sold out beforehand to *season*-ticket holders. The same stadium held 49,953 just a few years ago for a *high school* football game. The annual October brawl between the University of Texas and the University of Oklahoma is not played in Austin or Norman, but during the country's largest state fair in Dallas's Cotton Bowl, in State Fair Park, also scene of the New Year's Day extravaganza. Lamar Hunt's World

Championship Tennis Finals are played every spring at Reunion Arena in Dallas, and the city has hosted one of the stops on the Virginia Slims Tour for the past several years at SMU's Moody Coliseum. For golfers there is the Byron Nelson Golf Classic, the traditional start of the Texas Swing in the PGA Tour, which is held in early May at the Las Colinas Sports Club. Major League baseball is played by the Texas Rangers at Arlington Stadium with a capacity of 43,508. In basketball, the Dallas Mavericks play in the Reunion Arena. And the Southwest Conference, including nine universities, is headquartered in Dallas.

The safest time to jog the streets or drive on the cloverleafing freeways around Dallas–Fort Worth is Sundays right after kickoff during the Cowboys' fall season. The usual 3 P.M. start is convenient not only for national TV, but also for the churchgoing public. Sometimes referred to as the Buckle of the Bible Belt, Dallas is home to hundreds of faiths—including four churches each of which is the largest in its denomination anywhere. They are Highland Park Methodist, First Baptist, Highland Park Presbyterian and East Dallas Christian.

Dallas is known in other veins, too. It forever will carry the stigma of being the site of President Kennedy's assassination, November 22, 1963. Home of Texas' first Republican governor since Reconstruction, former Gov. Bill Clements, Dallas also hosted the 1984 Republican Convention. Dallas is the home of Neiman-Marcus, the specialty store that in 1987 will celebrate 80 years of class, panache, and extravagance. The Texas-size Dallas Market Center includes the Apparel Mart, the Decorative Center, the Home Furnishings Center, Market Hall, and the World Trade Center.

Though windier than Chicago and with more rain than Seattle, Dallas's weather is a big calling card for snowbirds coming in from the northern climes. Dallas rises early, but it bows out very late: After dinner at, perhaps, a classic French restaurant (visitors find there *is* life after chili, barbecue, and charbroiled steaks). Residents and visitors—children of all ages—frequent Six Flags Over Texas, a pioneer of the one-ticket amusement park, and a variety of other spreads.

Art to Art

Downtown Dallas is not noted for its nightlife, with the exception of the major hotels and its revitalized west end. While Fort Worth wins accolades for three world-class museums—the Amon Carter, Kimbell (whose acquisition budget is only surpassed in this country by that of the Getty Museum in California), and Science and History—Dallas makes headlines in the arts of symphony, opera, and theater, and especially the promising futures of each. In mid-1982 Dallas voters approved a $247-million bond issue,

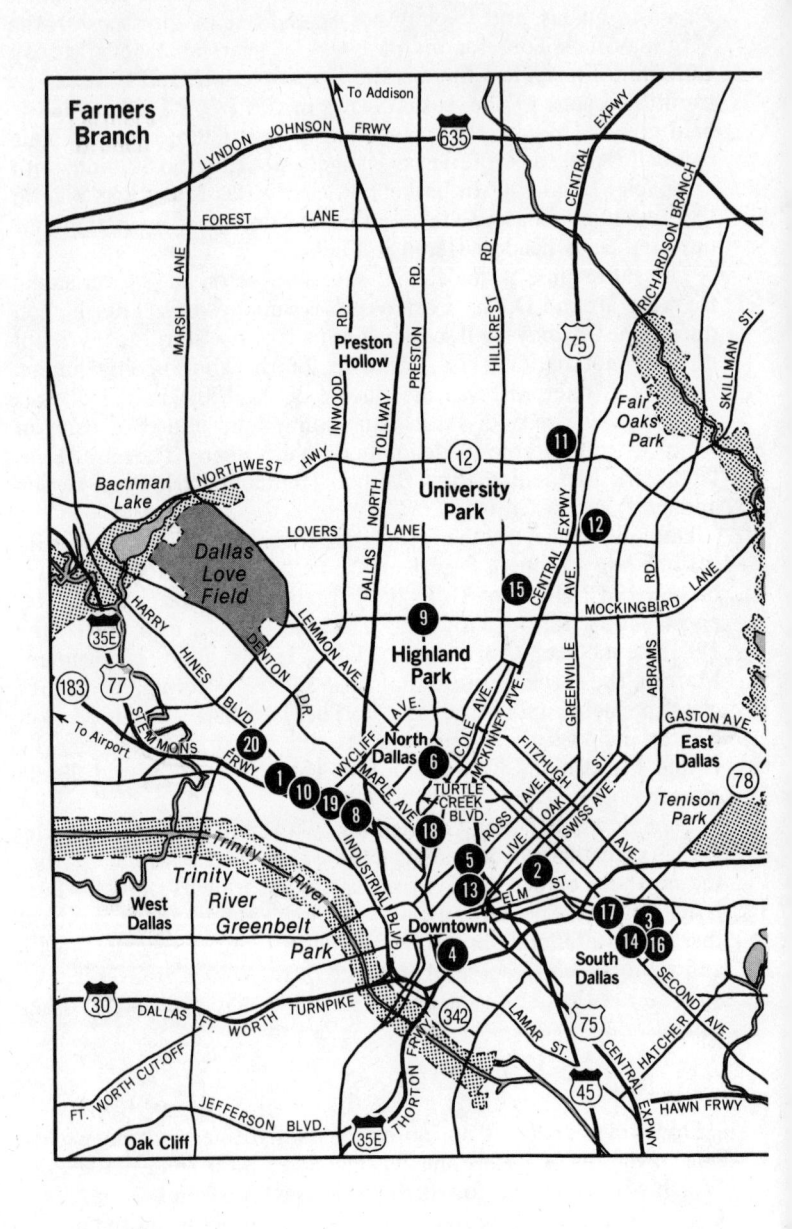

DALLAS AND FORT WORTH

DALLAS AND FORT WORTH

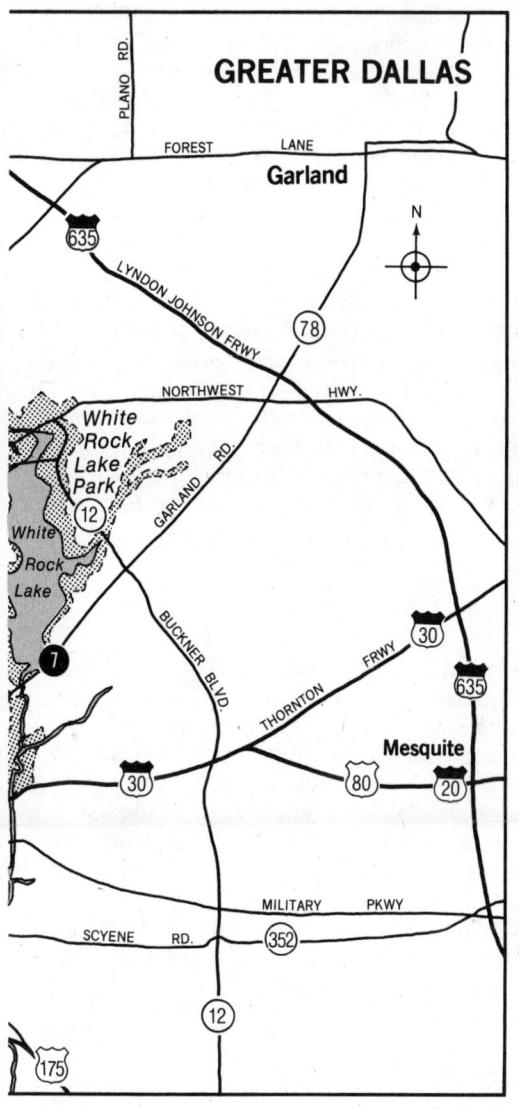

GREATER DALLAS

Points of Interest

1) Apparel Mart
2) Baylor University Medical Center
3) Cotton Bowl
4) Dallas Memorial Auditorium and Convention Center
5) New Dallas Museum of Art (Arts District under dev.)
6) Dallas Theater Center
7) DeGolyer Estate
8) Furniture Mart
9) Highland Park Shopping Center
10) Market Hall
11) NorthPark Center
12) Old Town Mall
13) Plaza of the Americas
14) Science Place
15) Southern Methodist University, including McFarlin Auditorium
16) State Fair Park, including the Dallas Museum of Natural History, Science Place/Southwest Museum of Science and Technology, Age of Steam Railroad Museum, Dallas Aquarium, Hall of State, Civic Garden Center, and Music Hall
17) Texas State Fair Grounds
18) Theatre Three
19) Trade Mart
20) University of Texas Health Science Center

which included $28.6 million for a new concert hall in the new downtown Arts District and $18 million to renovate more than a half dozen buildings, including museums, at State Fair Park. The same year Dallas opened its new $40-million downtown library and, in early 1984, the $40-million Dallas Museum of Art, in the Arts District with 210,000 square feet on 8.9 acres.

John Neely Bryan founded Dallas—named for Vice-President George Mifflin Dallas—in 1841 when he set up a trading post on the banks of the Trinity. But "culture" came to Dallas in 1855 with a party of 200 French, Swiss, and Belgians intent on founding a utopia. It's not certain what they thought they would find in the area to complement their efforts. They failed, but the scientists, artists, naturalists, writers, and musicians on the scene had dignified a frontier city. In 1873, the east-west line of the Texas & Pacific Railroad was completed through Dallas, crossing a railroad line reaching from Houston and making Dallas the first railroad crossing town in Texas.

Artists, writers, and musicians still call Dallas home, and along with their white- and blue-collar cohorts, they live in all corners of sprawling Dallas and its thriving suburbs and neighbors (don't let the names fool you: Plano, Grand Prairie, Mesquite, Farmers Branch), and in Oak Cliff, a scenic section of South Dallas where it's again becoming fashionable to live.

Friendly Rivalry

According to a study made by the University of Texas Graduate School of Business, Dallas, Houston, and Austin, in that order, are the most popular destinations when Texans travel within their state. (Fort Worth finished behind San Antonio and Galveston.) But a more interesting note is that, according to another study, Dallasites on the average travel to Houston, 250 miles to the south, more often than they do the 20-plus miles to Fort Worth on the other end of the Old Dallas–Fort Worth Turnpike (now I–30). The two cities are so close, yet so far apart.

Fort Worth, a city of close to 500,000, and Dallas have grown because of their persevering, industrious residents and, in some ways, despite them. Somewhere between Dallas and Fort Worth the line between east and west is drawn. Or, as the late Oklahoma humorist Will Rogers once put it: "Fort Worth is where the West begins and Dallas is where the East peters out." There has always existed a friendly rivalry between the two cities, but just how friendly depends upon whom you ask. Though competitive down to the latest concert or nightclub, the two have cooperated on planning and economics more than once—witness the Dallas–Fort Worth Airport—though it didn't happen overnight.

Sophisticated and fashionable Dallas is in a hurry; Fort Worth is more laid back. A well-dressed city, Dallas leans toward formalities; clean jeans and a jacket are accepted most anywhere in Fort Worth. But because most every building (and parts of many theme parks) is air-conditioned because of the summer heat, Dallas and Fort Worth are two cities where a businessman might take *off* his coat to go outside.

During World War II, both cities grew in population and wealth because of the defense industries, chiefly relating to airplanes, helicopters, and other such military products. After the war, Dallas became a leading producer of electrical and electronic equipment and, along with Fort Worth, a producer of aircraft and missile parts as well. In addition to its cattle-industry headquarters, Fort Worth is on the map with the aircraft, grain, and oil industries and as a mercantile and distribution center.

Where the West Begins

Though never a fort, Fort Worth was eventually named in honor of General William J. Worth, a Mexican War hero. Fort Worth got its start in 1849 as a military encampment protecting area settlers from Indians. Built on bluffs overlooking the Trinity River, it was perfect for watching over the sprawling prairie for Comanches. The view west from the Trinity bluffs soon changed to cattle on the Chisholm Trail, as cowboys drove their herds across Texas and Oklahoma to the Dodge City and Abilene, Kansas, stockyards.

Fort Worth was their last stop on the way north and their first stop on the way home during the cattle drives. A section of downtown, now occupied mostly by the Tarrant County Convention Center, grew into Hell's Half Acre, a shoot-'em-up haven of saloons, gambling houses, and brothels for the fun-seeking cowboys after their drives.

In 1876, Fort Worth elected "Long Hair Jim" Courtright as marshal and told him to keep peace in town but not to chase off the cowboys—or their money. Fast with his guns, he was an honored Civil War veteran and had toured with Buffalo Bill Cody's Wild West Show. With Hell's Half Acre calmed down but still stomping, Fort Worth saw many famous visitors, among them Doc Holliday, Wyatt Earp, and Butch Cassidy and the Sundance Kid. (A gambler himself, Courtright was gunned down on Main Street in 1887 by White Elephant saloon owner Luke Short, a retired cowboy.)

The *New York Daily Chronicle* reported in 1882: "Fort Worth is cosmopolitan. It has the rush and energy of a frontier town with strange contrasts of nationality. It smacks of Mexico and New York. Broadway and ranch brush against one another."

DALLAS AND FORT WORTH

DALLAS–FORT WORTH AREA

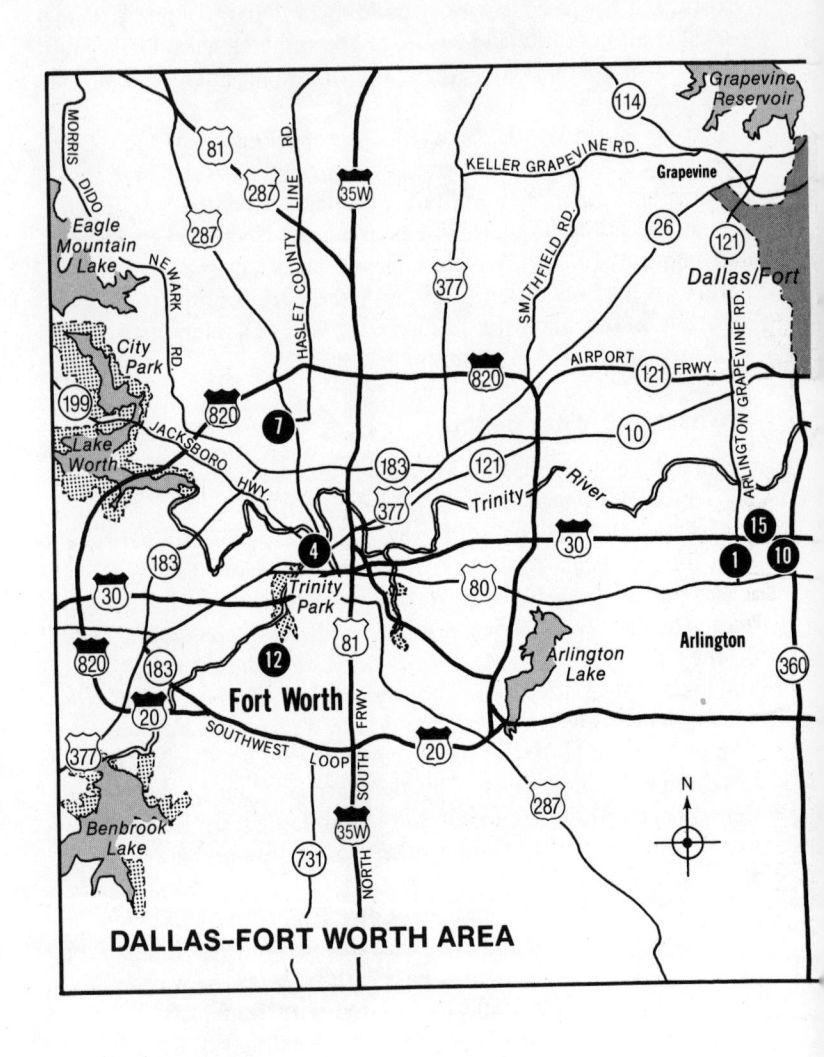

Points of Interest

Arlington Stadium, **1**
Dallas/Fort Worth Airport, **9**
Dallas Love Field, **2**
Downtown Dallas, **3**
Downtown Fort Worth, **4**
The Galleria, **5**
International Wildlife Park, **6**
Meacham Field Municipal Airport, **7**
Prestonwood Town Center, **8**

DALLAS AND FORT WORTH

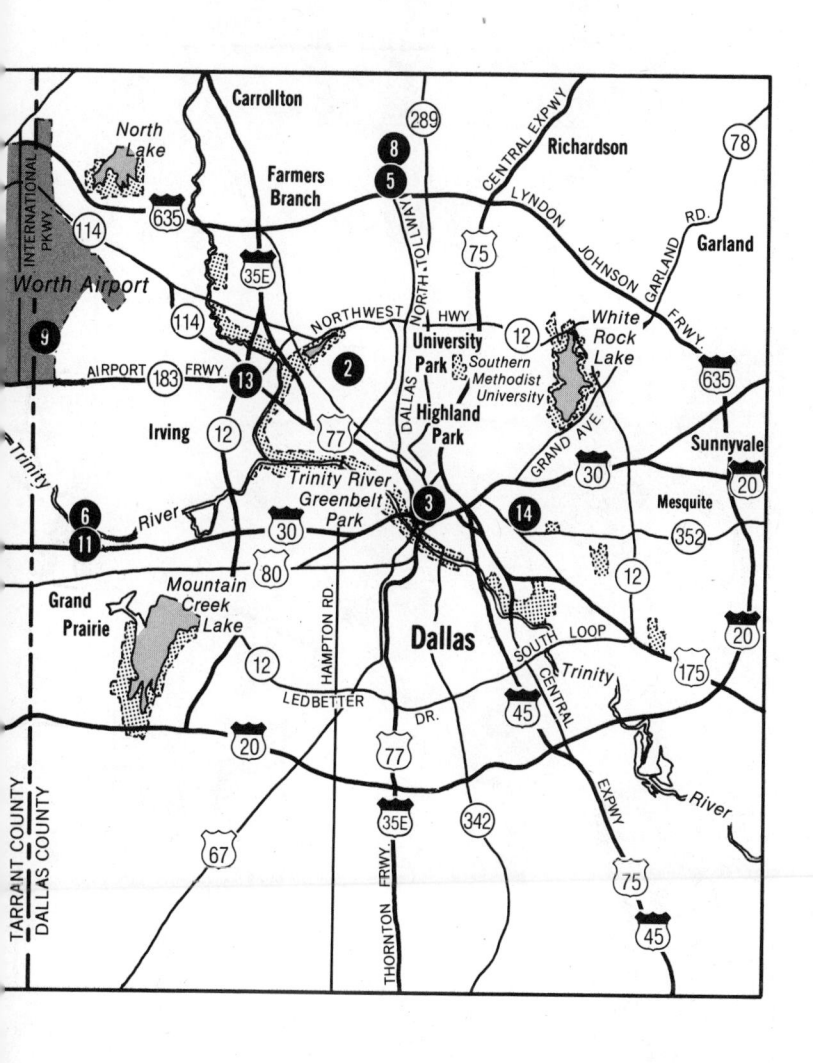

Six Flags Over Texas, **10**
Texas Christian University, **12**
Texas Stadium, **13**
Texas State Fair Grounds, **14**
Wax Museum of the Southwest, **11**
Wet 'n Wild, **15**

50   DALLAS AND FORT WORTH

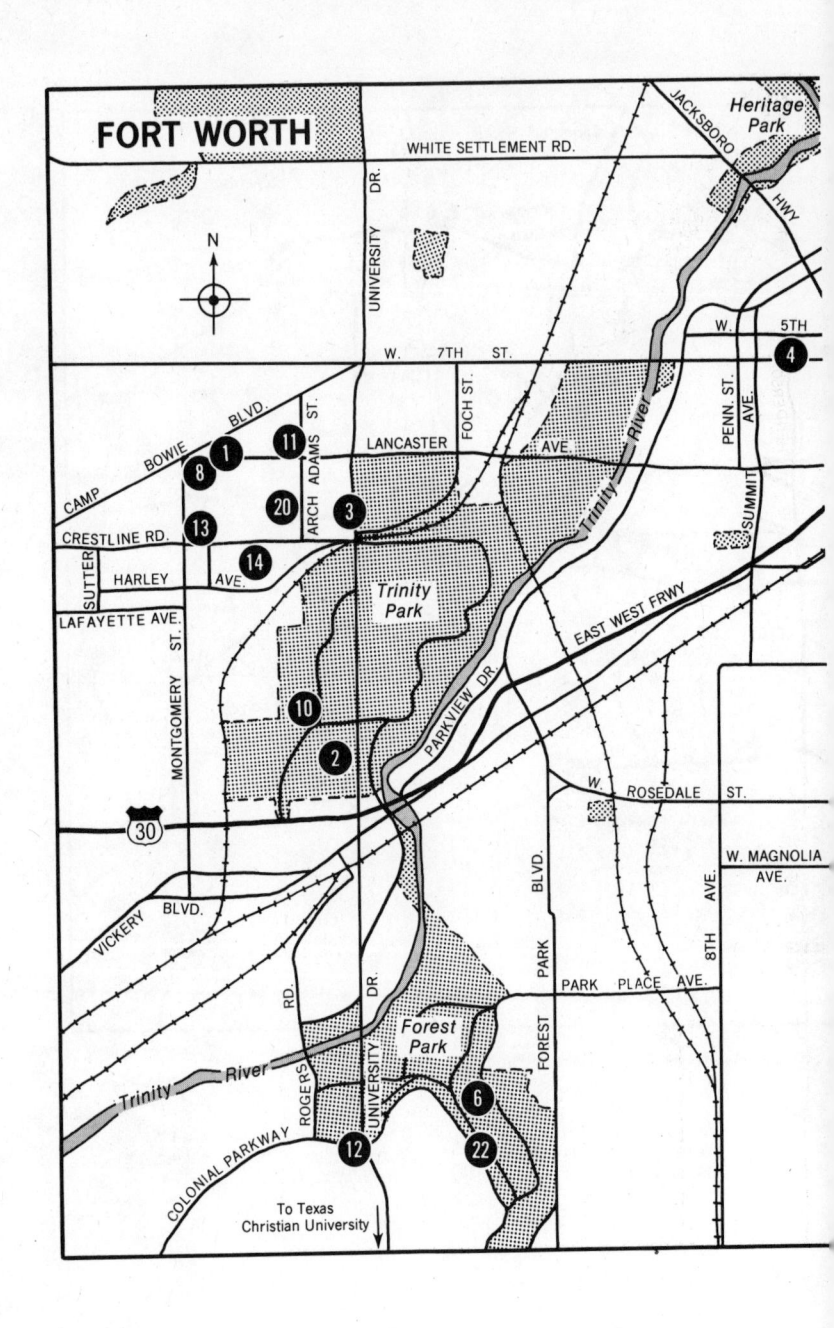

DALLAS AND FORT WORTH

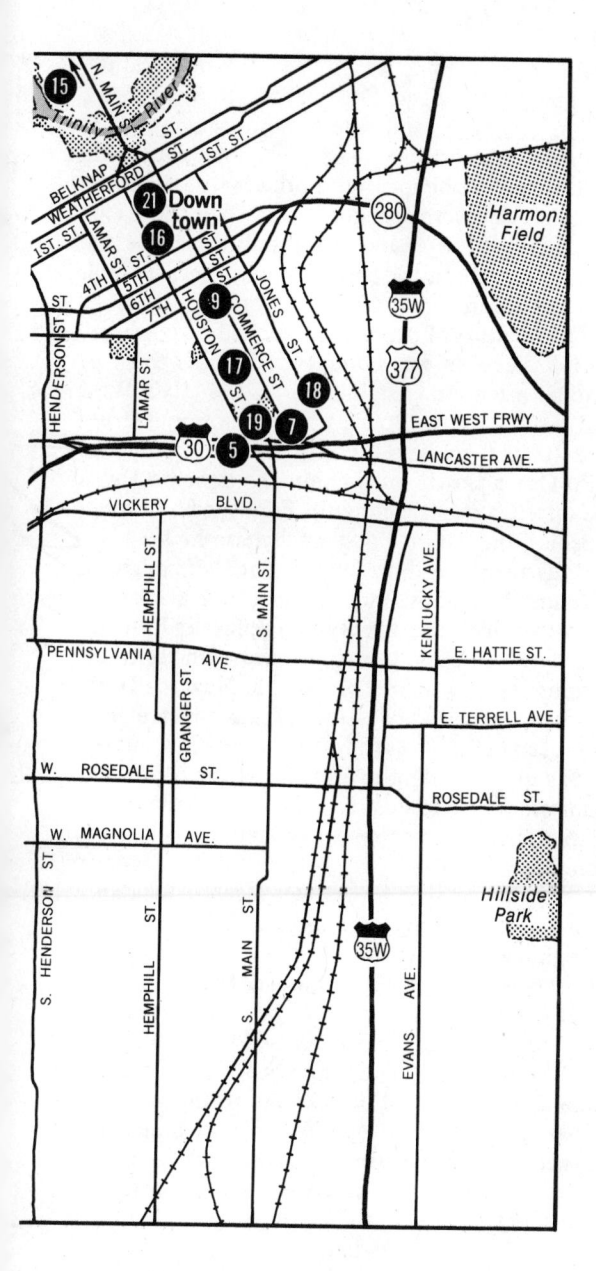

Points of Interest

1) Amon Carter Museum
2) Botanic Garden
3) Casa Manana
4) Cattlemen's Museum
5) Convention and Visitors Bureau
6) Forest Park Aquarium
7) Forth Worth Hilton
8) Fort Worth Art Museum
9) Hyatt-Regency
10) Japanese Garden
11) Kimbell Art Museum
12) Log Cabin Village
13) Museum of Science and Technology
14) Southwestern Exposition and Fat Stock Show Buildings
15) Stockyards
16) Sundance Square
17) Tarrant Country Convention Center
18) Train Station
19) Water Garden
20) Will Rogers Memorial Coliseum
21) Worthington Hotel
22) Zoological Park

Real Cowtown

Soon the railroads were stretching west into Fort Worth and the city entered into its boom-town stage. The Fort Worth Stockyards, second in size only to Chicago's, and several meatpacking houses sprang up at the turn of the century. The town soon earned its other nickname, Cowtown. Longhorns and other cattle filled the stockyards, and buffalo skins were brought in from West Texas for shipment north and east. Rodeos and stock shows became the order of the day. They're still on the scene today, in fact, at Will Rogers Memorial Center and in the revitalized Stockyards area.

After the turn of the century, Fort Worth still had its cowboys, cattle, and Hell's Half Acre but was no longer a frontier town. It was receiving national attention. Established on the city's West Side during World War I, Camp Bowie was an enormous army training facility for 100,000 soldiers. Shortly after the Armistice was signed in 1918, Camp Bowie finally shut the door on Hell's Half Acre. J. F. Cantrell began cleaning up Fort Worth himself, so to speak, by opening the nations' first washateria in 1934.

There was no oil discovered in Fort Worth, but there might as well have been. Hundreds of thousands of barrels of black gold headed for Fort Worth, which had twenty-two refineries by 1922. Oil companies' headquarters came to the city and with them lots of money. Big buildings sprang up in Fort Worth. Now the Hyatt Regency, the historical fourteen-story Hotel Texas—where John F. Kennedy spent his last night—was the direct result of oil money, as well as being the tallest building in Fort Worth in 1921. The city is still headquarters for hundreds of oil and oil-related industries, including exploration development, wildcatters, petroleum equipment, and refining.

A slice of Fort Worth's present downtown facelift, Sundance Square, with its turn-of-the-century architecture, features restaurants, shops, and nightspots in low-rise buildings. The downtown rebirth includes three new luxury hotels, Sundance Square, and the Water Gardens and has been ongoing since the early 1970s.

Downtown Fort Worth is bounded by I-30, I-35W and the more scenic Trinity River, which makes a better name for itself in Cowtown, especially along Trinity and Forest Parks to the west and southwest. These parks are home to Fort Worth's celebrated Botanic and Japanese gardens and zoo, aquarium, and Log Cabin Village, respectively. Texas Christian University and Amon Carter Stadium are several more blocks south.

West of Trinity Park, culture thrives in the previously mentioned art museums and Casa Manana theater in the Will Rogers complex. On the wilder side of town, the Stockyards area is ten minutes north of the business district in the rejuvenated area north of downtown. Outside of downtown, shoppers congregate at Ridgmar Mall, west on I-30; at Hulen Mall, southwest of TCU on I-20; and at Northeast Mall, northeast on Texas 121 at Loop 820-in and near a sea of suburbs known as Haltom City, Richland Hills, North Richland Hills, Hurst, Euless, and Bedford.

PRACTICAL INFORMATION FOR DALLAS AND FORTH WORTH

HOW TO GET THERE. There are, of course, four conventional ways to get about in the United States: car, plane, bus, and train. If you plan to travel long distances, it is usually cheaper—in both time and price—to go by plane than by rail. For distances less than 300 mi., the train or bus is cheaper and may be faster, too. But rail service to Dallas-Fort Worth is limited to three times a week. As for calling your own shots, stops, and scenery, nothing beats a car—especially around Texas. And because public transit has not mastered the expansive Dallas-Fort Worth Metroplex, a car is a necessity within the area.

By air. Because new airlines and services are being added at Dallas-Fort Worth (midway between both cities) International Airport seemingly every month, travelers should consult the *Official Airline Guide,* published twice monthly, for the most current airline schedules and information. The area has come a long way since 1919, when America's first airline was started in Fort Worth by three men to fly gift packages of candy to surrounding towns. Love Field, Redbird Airport, and Addison Municipal Airport are Dallas's smaller airports. Love Field (670–6073) is a municipal airport in Dallas and offers an average of 115 daily scheduled flights on Southwest Airlines within Texas and surrounding states. Redbird (670–7612) in southwestern Dallas is also owned and operated by the city and serves private and commercial air traffic. Located 12 miles north of downtown is Addison Municipal Airport (248-7733), now one of the 10 busiest municipal airports in the nation. Opened in January 1974, Dallas-Fort Worth Airport, with 17,800 acres, is "larger than the island of Manhattan," as Texans are quick to point out. The airport, 17 mi. from the central business districts of both Dallas and Fort Worth, is one of the things highly competitive Dallas and Fort Worth have agreed upon. The acreage, lying within the boundaries of the cities of Grapevine, Euless, Irving, Coppell, and Tarrant County, was mostly low-yield farm and ranch land. Being one of the nation's largest and busiest, D/FW International Airport hosts about 23 airlines flying to points within Texas, the U.S., and all over the world. Airtrans, D-FW's automatic transit system, provides transportation from terminal to terminal, to and from remote parking areas, and to the on-site hotel (the Hyatt). There is a charge to use Airtrans, except from the remote parking lots (free). For information on the surface transportation system to Dallas and Fort Worth, see the *How to Get Around* section, below.

The approximate flight times to Dallas-Fort Worth Airport from these Texas cities are: Austin, 50 minutes; Brownsville-Harlingen, 1½ hours; El

Paso, 2½; Houston, 1; and San Antonio, 1. The approximate flight times from these U.S. cities are: Atlanta, 1½ hours; Miami, 3; Chicago, 2; Denver, 1½; Las Vegas, 2½; Los Angeles, 3; New York, 3; San Francisco-Oakland, 3½; Seattle, 3½; Washington, D.C., 2½. Flight time from London is 9; Frankfurt, 10, and Tokyo, 12.

Discounts are offered by many airlines to members of families traveling together. Thirty-day excursion fares, youth fares for college students, and special low fares (on a standby basis) for members of the armed forces are also offered by many airlines. Most of the fares have certain restrictions, such as requiring the traveler to make the trip during certain times of the week, principally to avoid those days when traffic is heavy. Discounts change frequently; savings can range from 15 to 45% over regular coach fare, so check with a travel agent or airline for the exact rates.

For more information on the Dallas-Fort Worth International Airport, write P.O. Drawer DFW, Dallas-Fort Worth Airport, TX 75261 (574–8888).

By bus. *Greyhound/Trailways* offers extensive route systems and schedules. Travelers from all U.S. areas can find easy access to the Dallas-Fort Worth Metroplex. Check with a travel agent or a nearby Greyhound/Trailways office for details on special tours and unlimited travel passes offering Dallas-Fort Worth as a destination, turnaround, or brief stop. The great distances involved in travel to and around Texas could make these passes very advantageous. Under the same ownership, the Trailways and Greyhound bus lines are found in the same Dallas terminal at 205 S. Lamar at Commerce. For scheduling and fares call 742–2002 or 741–1481. In downtown Fort Worth, the Trailways bus terminal is at 901 Commerce, the Greyhound terminal at 1005 Commerce. Numerous other terminals are used in and around both cities, including the Mid-Cities and other suburban areas.

By train. Amtrak services both Dallas (653–1101, 10 AM–5:30 PM) and Fort Worth (336–1010) on a limited schedule. The toll-free number for both cities is (800) 872–7245. The Amtrak Eagle Route originates in Chicago and stops in Dallas three afternoons a week (Monday, Wednesday, and Saturday) before going through Ft. Worth the same days on its way southward to San Antonio, where connections are available to Los Angeles. The return trip arrives in Fort Worth each Tuesday, Friday, and Sunday afternoon on its route eastward to Dallas and eventually Chicago. Consult a travel agent or Amtrak for details on excursion-and family-fare structures, and discounts for senior citizens and the handicapped. The Amtrak passenger station in downtown Dallas is at Union Station, 400 S. Houston (at Young) near the Hyatt Hotel and Reunion Tower; in Fort Worth, at 15th and Jones.

By car. Whether in the traveler's own vehicle or a rental, the easiest access to and around the Metroplex is by car. Major attractions in Dallas and Fort Worth are spread throughout the area, and the two cities are 28 mi. apart on either end of the Old Dallas-Fort Worth Turnpike—now officially I-30 with free access. Interstate highways—I-35E (north-south through Dallas) and I-35W (north-south through Fort Worth), I-30, and I-20—connect Dallas and Fort Worth to the rest of the country.

The approximate drive times to Dallas-Fort Worth from these Texas cities are: Austin, 3½ hours; Brownsville-Harlingen, 10; El Paso, 11; Houston, 5; and San Antonio, 5.

DALLAS AND FORT WORTH 55

Most major car-rental companies have outlets at the Dallas-Fort Worth International Airport, Dallas Love Field, and numerous locations in and around Dallas, Fort Worth, the Mid-Cities, and the suburbs. For reservations, refer to these toll-free numbers: *Avis,* (800) 331–1212; *Budget,* (800) 527–0700; *Dollar Car Rental,* (800) 421–6868; *Hertz,* (800) 654–3131, and *National,* (800) 328–4567. Taxi service available in the Dallas area is listed in the Yellow Pages and includes *Yellow Cab of Dallas* (214) 426–6262, *Terminal Cab* (214) 350–4445, *Taxi Dallas* (214) 631–8588, and *State Taxi* (214) 823–2161 (doesn't serve airport). For transportation for the disabled call *HandiRides* (214) 658–6200 (except for the airport), *American Cab* (214) 946–9999, or *Dallas Handicapped Services* (214) 744–3600.

TELEPHONES. The area code for Dallas County is 214; for Tarrant County (Fort Worth), 817. The following cities and suburbs are **214:** Dallas, Grand Prairie, Irving, Farmers Branch, Carrollton, Lewisville, Renner, Addison, Richardson, Plano, Garland, Wylie, Rowlett, Mesquite, De-Soto, Duncanville, and Cedar Hill. The following cities and townships are **817:** Fort Worth, Richland Hills, North Richland Hills, Haltom City, Grapevine, Euless, Hurst, Bedford, Arlington, Mansfield, Crowley, Benbrook, and Cresson.

You do not need to dial the area code if it is the same as the one from which you are dialing. Local directory assistance in either city is simply 1411. An operator will assist you on person-to-person, credit-card, and collect calls if you dial "0" first. From outside the 214 area-code region, directory information for Dallas can be obtained toll-free by dialing 1–214–555–1212. From outside the 817 area-code region, directory information for Fort Worth can be obtained toll-free by dialing 1–817–555–1212. In either case, ask the operator if the party you need to call has a Metro number that can be dialed free from anywhere in the Dallas-Fort Worth Metroplex. Dial 1–800–555–1212 to see if there is an 800 toll-free number for the business you want to reach.

Emergency Numbers. In Dallas proper: *emergency* ambulance, police or fire, 744–4444; Parkland Hospital emergency room, 590–8281. In Fort Worth proper: *emergency* ambulance, 335–4357; fire, 332–2131, and police, 335–4222. John Peter Smith Hospital, 921–3431. Or, dial "0" for Operator, and ask the person's help in connecting you immediately with the appropriate agency. Please note that these are for *emergency* use only.

HOTELS AND MOTELS in Big D (from Oak Cliff to Far North Dallas), Fort Worth, and the Mid-Cities and D-FW Airport areas cater to a wide variety of tastes and pocketbooks. We offer only a selection of convenient hotels and motels. New facilities are opening almost every month, and many others are undergoing expansions, additions, or restorations. Dallas hosts over two million convention visitors annually, helping to make the city the number one visitor destination in Texas, so be sure to reserve your rooms as soon as your travel plans are set.

A free publication from the Dallas Convention & Visitors Bureau (see *Tourist Information,* below) lists dozens of discount packages offered by some of the city's most luxurious hotels, as well as modestly priced accommodations. Many packages are geared around the weekend or sporting events. For more information on lodging in the Fort Worth area, contact the Fort Worth Convention and Visitors Bureau (see *Tourist Information*). With rare exceptions, all lodgings in the Metroplex are air-conditioned, and most have swimming pools. Rates may be higher during the State Fair (October) and Cotton Bowl week (New Year's Day and the week preceding). Most hotels near Six Flags charge higher rates when the park is open daily (summer). Weekend rates at some hotels are as much as 50% lower.

Hotel rates are based on single occupancy in a regular double-bed room. Categories determined by price are: *Super Deluxe,* $110 and up; *Deluxe,* $90 to $109; *Expensive,* $80 to $89; *Moderate,* $70 to $79; *Inexpensive,* $60 to $69; and *Basic Budget,* less than $60. All rates are subject to change with inflation. All hotels are in alphabetical order by price category and represent only a sampling.

DFW Airport/Mid-Cities Area

Super Deluxe

The Dallas Marriott Mandalay at Las Colinas. 221 E. Las Colinas Blvd. at Texas 114, in Irving's Las Colinas Urban Center; (214) 556-0800. Ten minutes from DFW Airport, 5 minutes from Texas Stadium, 15 minutes from downtown Dallas, 28 stories. Opened in summer 1982. Three restaurants, including Enjolie, and a club; outdoor pool, Jacuzzi, steam room, jogging track, and workout room. AE, DC, MC, V.

DFW Airport Marriott. 8440 Freeport Pkwy., north entrance to DFW Airport; (214) 929-8800. Seven minutes from airport. Free shuttle service. Opened October 1982. Two restaurants, two clubs, indoor/outdoor pool, exercise room, whirlpool, and sauna. AE, DC, MC, V.

Hyatt Regency DFW. In the center of DFW Airport area; (214) 453-8400. Formerly the Amfac Hotel and Resort; 1,390 rooms, four restaurants, two clubs with equipment room, tanning room, nutritional analysis, indoor/outdoor pool, shuttle bus to Bear Creek (36-hole golf course, 10 racquetball courts, three indoor and four outdoor tennis courts.) AE, DC, MC, V.

Deluxe

DFW Hilton and Conference Center. 1800 Hwy. 26E, north entrance to DFW Airport; (817) 481-8444. Opened 1983; 401 rooms. Free shuttle service, and there is a courtesy phone. Health club with two indoor and six outdoor tennis courts, indoor/outdoor pool. 15 minutes from Grapevine Municipal Golf Course, basketball court, running track, near Austin Ranch (dude ranch).

Sheraton Grand Hotel. Texas 114 at Esters, 10 minutes north of DFW Airport; (214) 258-4900. Opened in 1982. Restaurant, two lounges, health club, sauna, steam, two racquetball and two tennis courts, indoor/outdoor pool. AE, DC, MC, V.

Moderate

Holiday Inn-DFW Airport North. 4441 W. Highway 114, Irving (five minutes from airport); (214) 929-8181. Extensively remodeled. Restaurant, bar, outdoor pool, exercise room. AE, DC, MC, V.

Inexpensive

Holiday Inn-DFW Airport South. 4440 W. Airport Freeway (Texas 183), Irving; (214) 399-1010. Recently remodeled. 408 rooms. Two restau-

DALLAS AND FORT WORTH

rants, one bar. Health club, with sauna, whirlpool, indoor/outdoor pool, miniature golf, pool tables. AE, DC, MC, V.

Basic Bargain

Days Inn. 2200 E. Airport Freeway (Texas 183), Irving; (214) 438–6666. Near Texas Stadium, 10 miles from airport. Restaurant, outdoor pool, AE, DC, MC, V.

Holiday Inn-Texas Stadium. 1930 E. Airport Freeway (Texas 183); (214) 438–1313. Restaurant, bar, outdoor pool. Free shuttle service (10 miles east of airport). AE, MC, V.

La Quinta-DFW Airport. 4105 W. Airport Freeway (Texas 183), Irving; (214) 252–6546. Ten minutes from airport with free shuttle service. Bar, 24-hour restaurant next door, outdoor pool. AE, MC, V.

Ramada Inn-Airport. 120 W. Airport Freeway, Irving; (214) 579–8911. Two miles west of Texas Stadium and 10 miles from airport. Restaurant, bar, two outdoor pools. AE, DC, MC, V.

Ramada Inn-Grand Prairie. 402 Safari Parkway, on I-30, Grand Prairie; (214) 263–4421. Across from wax museum and 10 minutes from amusement parks. Restaurant, club, and outdoor pool. AE, DC, MC, V.

Dallas Area

Super Deluxe

Adolphus Hotel. 1321 Commerce St., downtown; (214) 742–8200. $45-million restoration complete. Built by brewer Adolphus Busch in 1912, marketed now as "a beautiful lady with a past." Spacious rooms. Three restaurants, including the celebrated French Room; three bars. Guests use nearby health spa, "The Texas Club," (J.R.'s club) with pools, basketball courts, jogging, classes, racquetball, Jacuzzi, sauna. AE, DC, MC, V.

The Fairmount. 1717 N. Akard at Ross, downtown; (214) 720–2020. This Dallas outpost of the venerable hotel chain offers 551 rooms in two towers. Three restaurants, including the elegant Pyramid Room and the Venetian Room for dinner show, and two bars (one with nightly entertainment), outdoor pool. Guests have unlimited use with $10-a-day pass of adjacent fitness facility. AE, DC, MC, V.

Four Seasons Hotel & Resort. 4150 N. McArthur Blvd., Las Colinas; (214) 717–0700. 315 rooms. Same property as the Tournament Player's Course (TPC) which is home to Byron Nelson Golf Classic (May 9–15). Two restaurants, two lounges, indoor racquetball, squash, tennis, track, classes, sauna/steam. AE, DC, MC, V.

The Grand Kempinsky. 15201 Dallas Pkwy., in the Quorum at Belt Line Road; (800) 527–1690 for reservations worldwide or (800) 442–2039 and (214) 386–6000 in Texas. Two restaurants, one lounge. 510 large rooms, including 40 suites. Adjacent to Prestonwood Town Center and Sakowitz Village Shopping. Gracious service, gleaming atrium lobby. Indoor/outdoor pool, exercise room, tanning room. AE, DC, MC, V.

Hotel Crescent Court. 400 Crescent Court; (214) 871–3200. On the edge of downtown. The focal point of the Crescent development (adjoining offices, shops, and galleries), the hotel features 190 rooms and 28 suites. The casually elegant Beau Nash restaurant is lobby level. Outdoor pool, spa, workout room. Free shuttle service around downtown. AE, MC, V.

Hyatt Regency Dallas. 300 Reunion Blvd., southwest downtown, next to Reunion Tower and across the street from Reunion Arena; (214) 651–1234. 19-floor atrium. 943 suites. Three restaurants, three bars, health club, jogging track, two tennis courts, sauna, outdoor pool, Jacuzzi. AE, DC, MC, V.

Loew's Anatole Dallas. 2201 Stemmons Freeway (I-35E), in Market Center; (214) 748–1200. A trio of glass pyramids covers two atria of trees and tapestries, with a 27-story adjoining tower. 1,620 rooms (145 suites), 16 restaurants and bars. Veranda health club, racquetball, tennis, indoor/outdoor pool, sauna, whirlpool, eucalyptus inhalation room, indoor/outdoor jogging track. AE, MC, V.

The Mansion of Turtle Creek. 2821 Turtle Creek Blvd., (214) 559–2100. Situated on a 4½-acre estate on the tree-lined creek of the same name, this mansion has 129 rooms and 14 suites, two dining areas, including the elegant Turtle Creek Restaurant. Belongs to Brookhaven Golf and Tennis Club (make reservations) 10 minutes away. Fully equipped new health club nearby. Limo service within three-mile radius of hotel. AE, DC, MC, V.

Plaza of the Americas. 650 N. Pearl Blvd., downtown; (214) 747–7222. This Trusthouse Forte property is on the west side of three towers connected by an atrium with shops, restaurants, offices, and an ice rink. Two restaurants, including Cafe Royal (French), and three bars. AE, DC, MC, V.

Sheraton-Park Central. 12720 Merit Dr., near LBJ Freeway (I–635) at Coit Road, near Olla Podrida shopping; (214) 385–3000. Opened late 1982. 550 rooms. Three restaurants, three lounges. Athletic Club within complex. AE, DC, MC, V.

The Westin Hotel. 13340 Dallas Pkwy. at LBJ Freeway (I-635), in the Galleria; (214) 934–9494. 440 rooms. Two restaurants, lounge, weights, jogging, outdoor pool, dry saunas. Use of adjacent fitness club.

Deluxe

Dallas Marriott-Park Central. 7750 LBJ Freeway (I-635) at Coit Road; (214) 233–4421. Near Olla Podrida shopping. Partially renovated with 445 rooms, restaurant, two lounges, outdoor pool, hot tub, exercise room. AE, DC, MC, V.

Doubletree Hotel. 5410 LBJ Freeway (I–635) at Dallas Parkway; (214) 934–8400. In Lincoln Centre. 509 rooms. Opened in 1982, with two restaurants, lounge, indoor/outdoor pool, Jacuzzi, two tennis courts. Use of adjacent fitness facility with racquetball, track, weights, basketball, sauna. AE, DC, MC, V.

Doubletree Hotel. 8250 N. Central Expressway (US 75) at Caruth Haven; (214) 691–8700. In Campbell Centre. 302 rooms. Near the Greenville Avenue restaurants and clubs and NorthPark and Old Town shopping. Princeton Grill and Lobby Bar, two tennis courts, putting green, shuffleboard, four Jacuzzis. AE, DC, MC, V.

Embassy Suites Hotel. 2727 Stemmons Freeway (I-35 E); (214) 630–5332. All-suite hotel near Market Center. Restaurant, bar, indoor pool, Jacuzzi, sauna. 248 rooms. AE, DC, MC, V.

The Omni-Melrose. 3015 Oak Lawn Ave., just northwest of downtown; (214) 521–5151. A small hotel built in 1924. Totally renovated. Restaurant

DALLAS AND FORT WORTH

and bar, 184 rooms. Affiliated with health facility, across from shopping, restaurants, bars. AE, DC, MC, V.

Sheraton-Dallas. 4100 N. Olive at Live Oak, downtown; (214) 922-8000. After a $45-million renovation, this popular chain is gaining new friends. Three restaurants, three bars, weight room. 500 rooms. AE, MC, V.

Expensive

Crown Plaza-Holiday Inn. 4099 Valley View Lane, at LBJ Freeway (I-635), Midway; (214) 385-9000. Luxury inn, with atrium, restaurant, lounge, whirlpool, exercise room, indoor/outdoor pool, sauna, adjacent track. AE, DC, MC, V.

Dallas Hilton. 1914 Commerce St., downtown, near Convention Center; (214) 747-7000. 746 rooms, two restaurants, two bars, and two hot tubs. AE, DC, MC, V.

The Dallas Parkway Hilton. 4801 LBJ Freeway (I-635) at Inwood Road; (214) 661-3600. Near Galleria shopping. Restaurant, bar, indoor/outdoor pool, $7 entrance to nearby health club. AE, DC, MC, V.

Harvey House Hotel. 7815 LBJ Freeway (I-635) at Coit Road; (214) 960-7000. Near Olla Podrida shopping. Rooms surround four courtyards. Restaurant, club, outdoor pool, Jacuzzi, and sauna. AE, DC, MC, V.

Hawthorn Suites. 7900 Brookriver Dr., Mockingbird at Stemmons; (214) 688-1010. All suites (97) in this Richardson and Arlington property. Complimentary buffet breakfast and cocktail hour, sport court, volleyball, basketball, jogging track, and outdoor pool. AE, DC, MC, V.

The Regent. 1241 W. Mockingbird Lane at Stemmons Freeway (I-35E), five minutes from Love Field; (214) 630-7000. Completely renovated, with 350 rooms, restaurant, bar. AE, DC, MC, V.

Stoneleigh Hotel. 2927 Maple Ave., just north of downtown; (214) 871-7111. Restaurant and bar, four tennis courts, outside pool. AE, DC, MC, V.

Stouffer Dallas Hotel. 2222 Stemmons Freeway; (214) 631-2222. 542 rooms. 30 guest stories. Two restaurants, four lounges, health club, outdoor heated pool, hot tub, sundeck, dry/wet sauna. Use of adjacent facility with tennis, racquetball, and track. AE, DC, MC, V.

The Summit. 2645 LBJ Freeway (I-635) at I-35E; (214) 243-3363. Convenient to both DFW and Love Field airports. Two restaurants, including Gabriel's, and a club, indoor pool, outdoor sauna. Use of adjacent facility with jogging, racquetball, weights, and classes, free. AE, DC, MC, V.

Moderate

Colony Parke Hotel. 6060 N. Central Expressway (US 75), near Mockingbird Lane; (214) 750-6060. Near Southern Methodist University. Restaurant, bar, coffee shop in garden setting. Indoor pool and sauna. 288 rooms. AE, DC, MC, V.

Dallas Hilton Inn. 5600 N. Central Expressway (US 75) at Mockingbird Lane; (214) 827-4100. Midway between downtown and LBJ Freeway (I-635), near Southern Methodist University. Three restaurants, including Trader Vic's and Harper's, and three bars, outdoor pool. AE, DC, MC, V.

Days Hotel. 1011 S. Akard St., just south of downtown, near Convention Center; (214) 421-1083. Restaurant, bar. 239 rooms. Indoor pool, exercise equipment. AE, DC, MC, V.

Hilton Richardson and Towers. 1981 N. Central Expwy. 12-story hotel with 250 rooms near South Fork and University of Texas at Dallas. Outdoor pool, sauna, workout room, two restaurants, lounge, nightclub. AE, DC, MC, V.

Holiday Inn-Downtown. 1015 Elm St., downtown; (214) 748-9951. 300 rooms, restaurant, lounge, outdoor pool, free weights. AE, DC, MC, V.

Marriott Market Center. 2101 Stemmons Freeway (I-35E), in Market Center; (214) 748-8551. 418 rooms, two restaurants, two bars, two outdoor pools, exercise room. AE, DC, MC, V.

Sheraton Inn-Mockingbird West. 1893 W. Mockingbird Lane, near Love Field; (214) 634-8850. Restaurant, club, including Las Vegas-style entertainment. Health club, hot tub, sauna, track, exercise equipment, outdoor pool, two racquetball courts.

Inexpensive

Bradford Plaza. 302 S. Houston at Jackson, downtown, opposite both courthouse and Union Station; (214) 761-9090. 117 rooms, restaurant, lounge, exercise room. AE, DC, MC, V.

Holiday Inn. 10650 N. Park Plaza; (214) 373-6000. Restaurant, bar, indoor pool, four tennis courts, health club. AE, DC, MC, V.

LeBaron Hotel. 1055 Regal Row at John Carpenter Freeway (Texas 183), across Trinity River from Texas Stadium; (214) 634-8550. Three restaurants, two clubs, two tennis courts, jogging track, outdoor pool, hot tub, weight room. AE, DC, MC, V.

Ramada Hotel. 3232 W. Mockingbird Lane, near Love Field; (214) 357-5601. Restaurant, bar, outdoor pool. AE, DC, MC, V.

Basic Bargain

Best Western Inn-LBJ. 8501 LBJ Freeway (I-635) at Coit Rd., (214) 234-2431. Near Olla Podrida shopping. Lounge, with restaurant next door, outdoor pool, miniature golf. AE, DC, MC, V.

Best Western-Market Center. 2023 Market Center Blvd., across from Market Center; (214) 741-5041. Restaurant, bar, outdoor pool. AE, DC, MC, V.

Boulevard Inn-Market Center. 2026 Market Center Blvd., (214) 748-2243. Restaurant nearby, outdoor pool. AE, DC, MC, V.

Holiday Inn-Market Center. 1955 Market Center Blvd., (214) 747-9551. Restaurant, lounge, outdoor pool. AE, DC, MC, V.

Holiday Inn-Northwest. 1735 S. I-35E, Carrollton and Farmers Branch; (214) 242-6431. Restaurant, bar. AE, DC, MC, V.

Howard Johnson's-Central. 10333 N. Central Expressway (US 75) at Meadow Rd.; (214) 363-0221. Near NorthPark shopping. Restaurant, bar, outdoor pool, four tennis courts, health club. AE, DC, MC, V.

Howard Johnson's-Market Center. 1955 Market Center Blvd., (214) 747-9551. Restaurant, lounge, outdoor pool. AE, DC, MC, V.

La Quinta-North Central. 4440 N. Central Expressway (US 75) at Henderson-Knox; (214) 821-4220. Restaurant nearby, outdoor pool. AE, DC, MC, V.

La Quinta-NorthPark. 10001 N. Central Expressway (US 75) at Meadow Rd.; (214) 361-8200. Near NorthPark shopping. Restaurant next door, outdoor pool. AE, DC, MC, V.

La Quinta-Northwest Farmers Branch. 13235 Stemmons Freeway (I-35E) at Valley View; (214) 620-7333. Restaurant nearby. AE, DC, MC, V.

La Quinta-Regal Row. 1625 Regal Row, off Stemmons Freeway (I-35E); (214) 630-5701. Restaurant nearby, outdoor pool. AE, DC, MC, V.

La Quinta-Richardson. 13685 N. Central Expressway (US 75) at Mid-Park Rd.; (214) 234-1016. Restaurant nearby, outdoor pool. AE, DC, MC, V.

Non-Smokers Inn. 9229 Carpenter Freeway (Texas 183); (214) 631-6633. One mile from Texas Stadium. Restaurants nearby, health spa, Jacuzzi, sauna, exercise gym, outdoor pool. AE, DC, MC, V.

Park Cities Inn. 6101 Hillcrest Ave., opposite Southern Methodist University; (214) 521-0330. Restaurant nearby. AE, DC, MC, V.

Quality Inn-Market Center. 2015 Market Center Blvd., (214) 741-7481. Restaurant, bar, outdoor pool, exercise room. AE, DC, MC, V.

Ramada Inn-Northwest. 13333 Stemmons Freeway (I-35E), Farmers Branch; (214) 241-8521. Restaurant, bar, outdoor pool, sauna, affiliated health club. AE, DC, MC, V.

Rodeway Inn-North Central. 4150 N. Central Expressway (US 75) at Fitzhugh; (214) 827-4310. Restaurant nearby, outdoor pool. AE, DC, MC, V.

Sheraton Inn-Northeast. 11350 LBJ Freeway (I-635) at Juniper Rd.; (214) 341-5400. Restaurant, bar, outdoor pool. AE, DC, MC, V.

Tropicana Inn. 3939 N. Central Expressway (US 75), near downtown; (214) 526-8881. Restaurant, lounge, outdoor pool, backgammon, AE, MC, V.

Valley View Inn. 6101 LBJ Freeway (I-635) at Preston Rd.; (214) 387-2525. Near Valley View shopping. Three restaurants, lounge with occasional entertainment, outdoor pool. AE, DC, MC, V.

Viscount Hotel. 4500 Harry Hines Blvd. (US 77); (214) 522-6650. In Market Center. Restaurant, bar, outdoor pool, transportation free to affiliated health club. AE, DC, MC, V.

Fort Worth Area

Super Deluxe

Hyatt Regency Fort Worth. 815 Main St., downtown; (817) 870-1234. Across from Convention Center. Building formerly the famous Hotel Texas. 520 rooms, two restaurants, three bars, outdoor pool, health spa, exercise room, weights. AE, DC, MC, V.

Worthington Hotel. 200 Main St., downtown; (817) 870-1000. In the middle of historic district. Formerly the Americana Hotel. Connected to Tandy Center shopping. 508 rooms, four restaurants, bar, exercise room, classes, indoor pool, two outdoor tennis courts, whirlpool, sauna. AE, DC, MC, V.

Moderate

Fort Worth Hilton Inn. 1701 Commerce St., downtown, near I-30; (817) 335-7000. Across from Water Gardens and near Convention Center; restaurant, bar, indoor pool, Jacuzzi. AE, DC, MC, V.

Inexpensive

Green Oaks Inn and Conference Center. 6901 West Freeway; (817) 738-7311. Next to a golf course; 282 rooms, restaurant, disco, two outdoor tennis courts, two outdoor pools, health club. AE, DC, MC, V.

Basic Bargain

Best Western Fort Worther. 4213 South Freeway; (817) 923-1987. 61 rooms, outdoor pool. AE, DC, MC, V.

Best Western Kahler West Branch Inn. 7301 West Freeway; (817) 244-7444. Formerly Best Western Tom Penny Inn. 120 rooms, restaurant, outdoor pool, kid's play area. AE, DC, MC, V.

Best Western Metro Center Hotel. 600 Commerce St., downtown; (817) 332-6900. 300 rooms, restaurant, lounge, exercise room. AE, DC, MC, V.

Days Inn-West. Las Vegas Trail, in White Settlement; (817) 246-4691. 120 rooms, restaurant, complimentary breakfast, outdoor pool. 30 minutes from Six Flags. AE, DC, MC, V.

Drummer's Inn-North. 2520 N.E. 28th St.; (817) 624-3104. 52 rooms, outdoor pool. AE, DC, MC, V.

Holiday Inn Midtown. 1401 S. University Dr.; (817) 336-9311. 182 rooms, restaurant, lounge, outdoor pool, exercise room. AE, DC, MC, V.

La Quinta-Fort Worth West. 7888 I-30; (817) 246-5511. 106 rooms, adjacent restaurant, outdoor pool. AE, DC, MC, V.

Park Central Hotel. 10 Houston St., downtown; (817) 336-2011. 120 rooms, restaurant, bar, outdoor pool. AE, DC, MC, V.

Quality Inn South. 4201 South Freeway; (817) 923-8281. 98 rooms, restaurant, outdoor pool. AE, DC, MC, V.

Ramada Inn. Junction of Texas 183 and I-820, Hurst; (817) 284-9461. Restaurant, club, outdoor pool, nearby athletic club. AE, DC, MC, V.

Ramada Inn Central. 2000 Beach St.; (817) 534-4801. 310 rooms, two restaurants, bar, outdoor pool. AE, DC, MC, V.

Rodeway Inn. 1111 W. Lancaster; (817) 332-1951. 120 rooms, restaurant club, indoor pool, hot tub, two saunas. AE, DC, MC, V.

HOW TO GET AROUND. Airport. Dallas-Fort Worth International Airport is about 17 mi. from the central business districts of both Dallas to the east and Fort Worth to the west, and, depending upon traffic, a 20- to 35-minute drive in either direction. Five main ground transportation services are available: *Super Shuttle* vans provide transportation (leaving every 15 minutes from the airport) to and from D/FW International Airport and home, office, or hotels in Dallas and Fort Worth. General reservation number is 329-2025 (requires one hour advance reservation). From D/FW International punch 02 on Ground Transportation Boards at the baggage claim areas to access the shuttle. Fares are determined by zip code. To a downtown Dallas residence the fare is $10, $6 for each additional passenger; to a North Dallas residence the fare is $15, $7 for each additional rider. To downtown hotels the fare is $8 and to North Dallas hotels the fare is $11. There is a van for the disabled; call ahead. *Tours by Stan* (TBS) (214) 361–7637 operates vans from D/FW International to downtown Dallas and Market Center every 15 minutes for $8. From major Dallas hotels TBS runs every 30 minutes to the airport. *Bluebird Van Service* (214) 267–4101 runs daily every 30 minutes to an hour charging $8 to downtown Dallas. *Flagship Services Vans* (214–259–1186) run every 30 minutes daily from the airport. *VIP Transport* (214–363–2067) is another van service that runs every hour daily (more frequently during conventions) for $8–$10 to downtown Dallas, Market Center, and N. Dallas. Taxis are metered (about $20 to downtown Dallas or $22.50 Fort Worth), plus tip, and a 50¢ surcharge for each additional passenger). Getting from terminal to terminal and in and out of the airport can be a motorist's dream. But the 30-minute drive between the airport and downtown Dallas can prove much longer if attempted around the time of a Dallas Cowboys football game. City streets are usually deserted at game time, except on or near both Texas 183 and 114, the south and north routes, respectively, from D-FW Airport to Dallas and two of the byways running right by Texas Stadium. General assistance number including multilingual information at the airport: 574–4420.

Dallas transportation. Dallas Area Rapid Transit (DART) 601 Pacific main office, (214) 748–DART for route information) operates citywide air-conditioned buses, with varied service on major routes throughout 15 Dallas-area communities. (75¢ exact change for first zone, $1.50 for second, $1.75 for third, and $2.25 for fourth zone fares). The downtown Hop-A-Bus shuttles (35¢ exact change) operate during business hours Monday through Friday, and half day on Saturdays with downtown, west end, and McKinney shuttle service Thursday through Saturday nights, a bus calling at each Hop-A-Bus stop every 5–12 minutes depending on the route. Three routes are available: The Blue Route (downtown library and City Hall), the East-West Main St. Red Route, and the more northern Green Route. Commuters and visitors weary of downtown parking-garage prices (upwards of $10 a day) can park all day in Lot E at Reunion Arena (southwest corner of downtown) for $1.50 and receive tickets good for round-trip rides to and from the central business district on Hop-A-Bus. Certain designated buses, equipped with wheelchair-lift service, serve some routes to major hospitals, clinics, and centers for the handicapped. Dallas Transit Bus Charters require 3-hour minimum and a 48-hour notice. Taxis (most air-conditioned) are metered ($2.20 for the first 1 mile, $1 for each additional mile, and 50¢ surcharge for each additional passenger). Several major taxicab services make pickups downtown, at major hotels and airports, and by phone from almost any location.

Fort Worth transportation. City Transit Service of Fort Worth, or simply Citran (2304 Pine, 870–6200), operates Fort Worth's air-conditioned buses, with daily service 6 A.M. to 9 P.M. on major routes (75¢ exact change, except in the downtown "free zone"). The Tandy Subday, a free ride, is the only privately owned subway in the world and Texas' only subway. The 7-minute round-trip ride runs about 1 mi. from a parking lot in the north of downtown to the Tandy Center. Taxis (most air-conditioned) are metered ($1.30 initially to first quarter-mile, $1 for each additional mile, and 50¢ surcharge for each additional passenger). Several taxicab services make on-street pickups downtown, at major hotels and D-FW airport, and by phone from almost any location.

By car. An automobile, whether you own or a rental one, is a necessity for taking in the Dallas-Fort Worth Metroplex (see *How to Get There,* above). Hint to drivers: Do not be confused by the oft-used terms "turnpike" and "tollway" in the Metroplex. What was the Dallas-Fort Worth Turnpike, running east and west between the two central business districts, is now part of I-30, and no toll is charged; the Dallas North Tollway, running north and south just northwest of downtown Dallas to just north of Belt Line, has doubled its toll to 50¢ to help finance an extension north.

On foot. A hint to walkers: As a safety precaution, both Dallas and Fort Worth police are quick to fine jaywalkers on downtown streets. Pedestrians should cross streets only in designated walks with the appropriate green signal light. Dallas has no subway system, but **Underground Dallas** affords downtown pedestrians the opportunity to park, shop, lunch, and bank without venturing out into the heat or cold. Entrances to the network of corridors may be found at the First International Building, One Main Place, and First National Bank for one segment, and Thanks-Giving Square and Republic Bank for another. The Underground is closed on Sunday and open only until 1:30 P.M. on Saturday.

TOURIST INFORMATION. Dallas. For free information, brochures, and booklets on Dallas and environs, contact the Dallas Convention & Visitors Bureau, Dallas Chamber of Commerce, Information Dept., 1201 Elm St., Dallas, TX 75270, (214) 746–6677. Hours are 8:30 A.M. to 5 P.M. weekdays. Walk-ins may find the chamber's other information center more accessible: The Dallas Visitors Information Center at Union Station (400 S. Houston St. in the southwest corner of downtown; (214)–747–2355) is open 9 A.M. to 5 P.M. daily.

Fort Worth. For free information, brochures, and booklets on Fort Worth and environs, contact the Fort Worth Convention & Visitors Bureau, 700 Throckmorton, Fort Worth, TX 76102; (817) 336–8791. The office is open 8:30 A.M. to 5 P.M. weekdays.

Mid-Cities. For more information on the Mid-Cities area, especially on theme parks and amusement centers and accommodations, contact the Arlington Convention & Visitors Bureau, City of Arlington, P.O. Box A, Arlington, TX 76010; (817) 265–7721, and the Grand Prairie Chamber of Commerce, 900 Conover St., Box 531227 Grand Prairie, TX 75053; (214) 264–1558.

Other sources. The Friday editions of the three major daily newspapers—the *Dallas Morning News,* the *Dallas Times Herald,* and the *Fort Worth Star-Telegram*—offer reams of information on local and area attractions, as do the monthly magazines *D* and *Texas Monthly.* The *Dallas Morning News* offers arts and entertainment information via a recorded telephone message: "Artsline, 522–2659," is operated 24 hours a day by the Dallas Arts Combine with assistance from the City Arts Program. It details activities and events on a rotating basis for more than 50 Dallas cultural organizations. The recording provides specific information on local music, dance, and theater events, free public performances, galleries, museums, and touring shows.

SEASONAL EVENTS. January. The *Cotton Bowl Classic and Parade,* usually staged New Year's Day in Dallas, draws a national TV audience. Revelers and families line the downtown streets for the free morning parade. And in early afternoon, football fans fortunate enough to secure tickets converge on the Cotton Bowl in State Fair Park (2 mi. east of downtown) for the bowl game between the Southwest Conference champion and another highly ranked college team. The only continuously held livestock show in the United States since 1896, the extravagant *Southwestern Exposition, Fat Stock Show, and Rodeo* warms Fort Worth, usually late-month and early February, with a combination of contests, rodeos, cowboys, carnivals, parades, and of course, people-watching.

February. The *Quaker State Open* tournament in Grand Prairie hosts the professional bowlers' tour and a stop on the *Virginia Slims Women's Tennis Circuit.* Amateur boxers compete in *Golden Gloves* tournaments in Fort Worth and Dallas, and runners hoof through the streets of Fort Worth for the *Cowtown Marathon.*

March. Dallas is the scene of the *Southwest Sports and RV Show,* the *Southwest Conference Basketball Classic XIII,* the *Gulf Goes Green St. Patrick's Day Celebration* and the *Dallas Home & Garden Show* at Market Hall.

April. Major-league baseball, of the American League's *Texas Rangers* variety, is uncorked early in the month (through early October) at Arlington Stadium, midway between Dallas and Fort Worth. Strollers and motorists take to the sidewalks and streets, especially along stately Turtle Creek in Dallas, to admire the *spring blooms* at their height around Eastertime highlighted at the Dallas Arboretum and Botanical Gardens. Lamar Hunt's *World Championship Tennis Finals* are staged in Dallas's Reunion Arena in late April or early May. And Traders' Village in Grand Prairie hosts a *Western Days Celebration and Rodeo.* At the end of April and into May, the *Grand Prix* speeds up at Fair Park.

May. The first weekend of the month, *Mayfest* in Fort Worth's Trinity Park offers arts and crafts, live entertainment, folk songs and dances, children's activities, sports and games, and lots of food. The Metroplex enjoys two stops on the Professional Golfers Association tour, the *Byron Nelson Classic,* now at Las Colinas in Irving, and the *National Invitation Tournament* at Colonial Country Club in Fort Worth. The Swiss Avenue Historical District, just east of downtown Dallas, holds its *tour of homes.* Dallas's *Artfest*—an event sponsored Memorial Day weekend at State Fair Park by 500 Inc., an organization that has donated more than $1 million to Dallas arts organizations—includes a juried art show, arts and crafts displays, and continuous entertainment.

June. The revitalized stockyards area north of downtown Fort Worth gets an added shot in the arm the second weekend with the *Chisholm Trail Roundup.* A parade, a trail ride, rodeos, historical tours, a chili cookoff, armadillo races, square dancing, street dances, and mock western gunfights commemorate the Chisholm Trail cattle drives from South Texas through Fort Worth to Abilene, Kan., in the late 1880s. Summer in both Dallas and Fort Worth is open season for *theater, musicals,* and *concerts.* Among the offering are: The Dallas Symphony Association's 10-week

Starfest at Park Central, with big-name stars all along the musical scale; musicals, from Dallas's State Fair Park Music Hall to Fort Worth's celebrated Casa Manana in Amon Carter Square; and *Shakespeare festivals* under the stars. June, July, and August are also the height of traffic on area *lakes* and in *theme parks and amusement centers.*

July. *Fireworks* shows on the Fourth of July light up the skies from Dallas's Cotton Bowl to various parks and lakes throughout the Metroplex.

August. Football fans dig out the binoculars and dust off the stadium seats for the *National Football League exhibition season* at Texas Stadium, but they really get serious in . . .

September, when the *Dallas Cowboys* begin their *de riguer* march to the National Football Conference playoffs. Area universities—including the Southern Methodist Mustangs, the Texas Christian Horned Frogs, the North Texas Mean Green, and the UT-Arlington Mavericks—take to their respective gridirons too. Fort Worth circles the last weekend for *Pioneer Days* in the Stockyards area for a carnival, a street shootout, handicrafts displays, a street dance, and a parade.

October. The *State Fair of Texas,* the biggest of its kind in the country, explodes with 17 days of entertainment, including a midway, exhibitions, contests, a rodeo, and a Broadway musical. State Fair Park is also the scene of the annual football battle between the University of Texas (Austin) and the University of Oklahoma (Norman) in the Cotton Bowl, also the stage for other college and high school games during that stint. Usually staid downtown Dallas rolls up its sleeves for *Cityfest,* a carnival of the arts. Public spaces and building lobbies are backdrops for musical productions, arts and crafts exhibits, ensembles, films, and demonstrations. Fort Worth reserves the first weekend for *Oktoberfest* at Tarrant County Convention Center, as the Symphony League's festival fills the arena and exhibit halls with a family-oriented schedule. Also on the calendar are the Dallas *Neiman-Marcus Fortnight,* an international salute to products from afar, *A Taste of Dallas's* best victuals, and the season tipoff at Reunion Arena (through spring) for the *Dallas Mavericks* of the National Basketball Association.

November. Runners and fast walkers take to the streets of downtown Dallas on Thanksgiving morning for the YMCA *Turkey Trot.*

December. The *White Rock Marathon,* takes place around and near this East Dallas lake. It's beginning to look a lot like Christmas early on as giant *Christmas trees* adorn both cities. And, looking like towering Yuletide presents from afar, downtown buildings in Fort Worth are outlined in lights.

FREE EVENTS. *The Dallas Morning News Artsline,* 522–2659, is a hotline detailing activities and events of more than 50 Dallas cultural organizations on a rotating basis, including arts and entertainment, music and dance, theater and free public performances, galleries and museums, touring shows, and others. It may be dialed 24 hours a day. Many events are free.

Regularly scheduled events in the area that are free to the public include parades—especially New Year's Day for the Cotton Bowl; in late January for the Southwestern Exposition, Fat Stock Show, and Rodeo (Fort Worth), and in October for the State Fair of Texas. Also, Shakespeare fes-

DALLAS AND FORT WORTH

tivals in summer, city festivals in spring and fall, and sidewalk symphonies during the year.

Most public parks, lakes, gardens, museums, and some historical sites charge no admission. See also *Participant Sports,* below.

TOURS. Dallas City Tours. *Gray Line* (4110 S. Lamar, Dallas, TX 75215; 824–2424), offers a variety of tours in and around the city. The latest sampling of tours includes All about Dallas, Southfork Ranch and J. R.'s Dallas, Dallas and Southfork, and—for groups of 30 or more—Texas BBQ, Six Flags Over Texas, Fort Worth—Where the West Begins, and A Day at a Texas Ranch. For prices, seasons of availability, and reservations, contact Gray Line. Tours may be boarded at these downtown locations: Dallas Hilton, 1914 Commerce; the Adolphus, 1321 Commerce; Holiday Inn, 1015 Elm St; Fairmont Hotel, Ross and Akard; Loew's Anatole and Marriott Market Center; and Hyatt Regency, 300 Reunion Blvd. and the Dallas Sheraton. Call for schedule.

American Tours gives general city tours and custom-designed tours of Dallas and Fort Worth. Costs vary with size of group and length of tour. Guide service can be provided. Call (214) 745–8939.

Dallas Surrey Services gives evening tours of the West End in a horse-drawn surrey; for a ride for up to 4 people, $15–$25, depending on length of ride. Call (214) 946–9911.

Fort Worth City Tours. *Gray Line* (3332 W. 7th St. in Fort Worth, 429–7563), shows the best of Fort Worth and environs. Tour sites include the Water Gardens, Tarrant County Convention Center, the Stockyards area, Chisholm Trail, Botanic Gardens, downtown, major art museums, Scott Theatre, and—in or near Dallas—the Southfork Ranch, Texas Stadium, downtown, JFK Memorial, Neiman-Marcus, Market Center, and—in or near Arlington—Six Flags Over Texas, American Airlines Academy, Arlington Stadium, and the Southwest Historical Wax Museum. For prices, seasons of availability, reservations, and gathering points, contact Gray Line.

The *North Fort Worth Historical Society* offers group tours of the Stockyards area, including visits to local shops, clubs, a cattle auction, and others. Rates are $4 per person with minimum rate of $40. Contact the society in the Stock Exchange Building, 131 E. Exchange Ave., Suite 115; 625–5082.

Other tours, inbound reception operators. For complete, up-to-date listings of tour and inbound reception operators in the Dallas area, write the Dallas Chamber of Commerce, Convention & Visitors Bureau, 1201 Elm St., Dallas, TX 75270; 746–6677. In the Fort Worth area, contact Fort Worth Convention & Visitors Bureau, 700 Throckmorton, Fort Worth, TX 76102; (817) 336–2491.

PARKS. As the site of the Texas Centennial Exposition in 1936, Dallas was the focus of the state's celebration of 100 years of independence from Mexico. Today, Fair Park's Centennial buildings comprise the largest collection of art-deco architecture in the U.S., and the site has recently been designated a National Historic Landmark. It is the center of Dallas's 6 municipal and private museums of history, science, and technology, and the setting for continuous events that make it Dallas's most heavily used cultural resource with over 5 million visitors annually. In preparation for the 1986 Texas sesquicentennial celebration, Fair Park enjoyed improvements costing a total $33 million. Site of the State Fair of Texas, the largest state fair in the nation, for 17 days each October, Fair Park offers 273 acres of entertainment, culture, and recreation just 2 mi. east of downtown Dallas via I-30; (214) 670–8795. Begun in 1904, the complex has housed several museums since 1936 (see *Museums,* below). Most facilities are open daily to the public, except during the fair. The Science Place (428–7200), $5 for adults, $2 for children; Civic Garden Center (428–7476), Aquarium (670–8441), Texas Hall of State (421–5136), or Museum of Natural History (670–8467). The Age of Steam Railroad Museum (421–8754) charges $2 for adults, $1 for children. Coming soon will be the African American Museum. The midway, with its nostalgic wooden roller coaster, is open weekends during the summer and, naturally, during the fair. State Fair Coliseum and the Cotton Bowl also are within the park. The Music Hall stages the Dallas Summer Musicals and the Metropolitan Opera, and the bandshell is site of the summer Shakespeare Festival. For information on what's happening at Fair Park, call 565–9931.

White Rock Lake. This Dallas lake is popular for sailing, picnicking, fishing, jogging, biking, hiking, people watching, and admiring mansions—including the late H. L. Hunt's on the west side. Bounded by Garland Road, Buckner Boulevard, and Northwest Highway in East Dallas, this city park is free. For information, call 321–2125. For more information on White Rock and other area bodies of water, see the *Lakes* section, below.

Old City Park, just south of downtown Dallas, features 36 restored buildings of the 1940s to 1910; (214) 421–5141; see the *Historic Sites* section, below.

Thanks-Giving Square is an oasis of grassy park, trees, and a chapel in the heart of downtown Dallas at the intersections of Bryan, Pacific, and Ervay. As business and traffic are negotiated at a frantic pace a few feet away, brownbaggers relax with associates at lunchtime amid the crimson crape myrtles of summer. The bells of thanksgiving may be heard during the noon hour weekdays and each half hour on weekends, recalling the reason for the park. Opened in 1977 to mark the 200th anniversary of the American Thanksgiving tradition, the square and its quiet chapel have been developed by the private interfaith Thanks-Giving Square Foundation. Philip Johnson designed the chapel, a white cube of Italian marble on a circle of red granite, and, inside, Gabriel Loire's stained-glass ceiling draws visitors' attention upward. Various religious and national holidays are observed throughout the year in services and programs. Open weekdays, 9 A.M. to 5 P.M.; weekends and holidays, 1 to 5 P.M. For information and schedules, call (214) 969–1977.

Fort Worth Nature Center and Refuge. 10 mi. northwest of downtown, via Texas 199 (the Jacksboro Highway) to Buffalo Road. Maintained by the city's parks and recreation department, this 3,400-acre wildlife habitat also offers 9 interpreted/marked nature trails, fishing, picnicking, and a visitor center. The wide variety of native habitats range from prairie and cross-timber forest to a lotus-marsh lake and river. Designated a national natural landmark, the center provides guided tours for prescheduled groups as well as many activities for the drop-in visitor. Naturalists at the Visitors Center can answer questions. A small herd of buffalo is maintained on a 50-acre range, as are several tame deer and a prairie-dog town.

Open daily, 8 A.M. to 5 P.M. weekdays, the refuge opens at sunrise on Saturdays, and 9 A.M. to 5 P.M. Sundays. Free. For guided-tour reservations for groups of 10 or more, call (817) 237-1111. No overnight camping is allowed.

Woodsy **Trinity and Forest Parks** off University drive in Fort Worth afford a beautiful drive or bicycle trip along the clear fork of Trinity River. The area includes parklands, pool, a zoo, rides, a miniature train and **Trinity Park Duck Pond,** where feeding the ducks is encouraged. Admission to the parks is free.

ZOOS. The **Fort Worth Zoological Park,** at 2727 Zoological Park Dr., off University Dr. south of I-30, has earned its wings and stripes. Its more than 850 species are housed in arrangements such as an African Diorama, and the James R. Record Aquarium and Herpetarium. The latter features one of the largest reptile exhibits in the world and the Aquarium houses a substantial variety of fresh- and saltwater fish and invertebrates, in addition to seals and sea lions. The Fort Worth Zoo Education Complex offers programs at 1 and 3 P.M. on weekends, its multimedia theater featuring an elaborate sound system. The zoo opens daily at 9 A.M.; closing hours vary. Adults $2, children $1.50, 25¢ and free, depending on age. Call (817) 870-7050 for more information. The **Forest Park Train,** with its 5-mi. jaunt lasting 45 minutes, is the world's longest miniature-train ride. From the entrance to the zoo, it runs summer months, Monday through Friday, 10 A.M. to 5 P.M., and Saturday and Sunday, 10 A.M. to 4 P.M. All ages, 90¢. Call (817) 923-8911.

The 50-acre **Dallas Zoo,** at 621 E. Clarendon Dr. in Oak Cliff, just 5 minutes south of downtown, offers more than 1,500 mammals, reptiles, and birds in a landscaped preserve, but its prairie-dog village near the entrance can keep many visitors distracted for at least a half hour. There is a huge flamingo exhibit. Breathing room at the small zoo is on the drawing boards: $30.4 million has been committed by voters to expand the zoo and create a new African-exhibit area called "Wilds of Africa," which will be opened July '89. The zoo is open daily Apr. 1–Sept. 30, 9 A.M. to 6 P.M., and the rest of the year, until 5 P.M. Adults $2, children age 6–11 $1.25, seniors $1.25, parking $2. Call (214) 946-5155 for information.

Dallas Aquarium: See the *Museums* section; below.

Fort Worth Nature Center and Refuge: See the *Parks* section, above.

GARDENS. The 114 acres of the **Fort Worth Botanic Garden,** off I-30 at University, offer 150,000 plants of more than 2,000 species. The majority of the tree-shaded (150 varieties) growths are a result of the garden's own seed and cuttings. Among the more than 200,000 guests a year are many blind visitors strolling through the Fragrance Garden. The garden of roses—some 4,000—is the site of many special events, especially weddings. The garden was built and landscaped during the Depression by 750 men, many working for meal tickets; the flagstone walks and shelter houses cost a mere $4,500. The project took 4,000 tons of rock. The garden, free to the public, is open daily, 8 A.M. to sundown. Call (817) 870-7686 for information.

The 7½-acre **Fort Worth Japanese Garden** in a corner of the Botanic Garden is a pleasant switch from the gravel pit and garbage dump formerly on the site. Built in the early 1970s, the garden offers a Meditation Garden, a Moon Viewing Deck, a Pagoda, and strolling gardens. Five bridges, three big pools, and authentic lanterns also adorn the landscape. The garden is open daily except Mondays 10 A.M.–5P.M., Nov. 1 through April. Summer hours (May 1 through Labor Day) are Tuesday through Sunday, 9 A.M.–7 P.M. The last ticket is sold 30 minutes before closing. Adults $1, except on weekends $1.50, students 5–19 50¢, under 5 free. Special tours can be arranged for adult groups of 10 or more in advance. Call (817) 870-7685.

The **Fort Worth Water Gardens,** 4.3 acres of south downtown real estate at I-30 and Main Street, draw thousands of visitors each year, in addition to the attention given them by movie companies (including the one that made *Logan's Run*), TV producers, dancers, singers, and brides. Philip Johnson and John Burgee of New York designed the park, built (a few hundred feet from the Chisholm Trail used 100 years ago) by the Amon G. Carter Foundation and presented to the city in 1974. Visitors can stand 38 ft. below ground level to experience 1,050 gallons of water per minute rushing down 710 feet of wall around the Active Water Pool, and nearby sheets of water flow silently down 22-ft. walls into a moat surrounding the Quiet Water Pool. The aerated-water pools use 40 nozzles to spray circular patterns over the pool. Though the plaza is open free 7–11:30 P.M. daily, water is activated from 9 A.M. to 4 P.M.

The **Dallas Civic Garden Center,** 1st and M.L. King Jr. Blvd., in State Fair Park, was begun in 1941. Its Tropical Garden Room houses tropical plants, a waterfall and pool with aquatic plants and tropical fish. The contemporary gardens outside include an herb-and-scent garden and, remarkably, a Shakespeare garden. Some displays include Braille. Lectures and seminars are commonplace at the center, open free Monday through Friday, 10 A.M. to 5 P.M., and Saturday, Sunday, and many holidays, from 12:30 P.M. Call (214) 428–7476 for information.

On 66 acres of rolling woodlands overlooking White Rock Lake in East Dallas, the **Dallas Arboretum and Botanical Society** provides a natural setting for visitors to meet horticulturists and other garden enthusiasts. For more information, contact the society, 8617 Garland Road, (214) 327-8623.

THEME PARKS AND AMUSEMENT CENTERS. The Dallas-Fort Worth area is a "big spread" for the first-time visitor trying to maneuver cloverleafing freeways and endless roads, some known by three and four names apiece. So the centrally located concentration of theme parks and amusement centers in Arlington and Grand Prairie is a blessing. The only problem is that once little Johnny sees one, he'll want to see them all.

Between Dallas and Fort Worth along I-30 (also known as the old Dallas-Fort Worth Turnpike) are:

Six Flags Over Texas. 2201 Road to Six Flags near Arlington Stadium, in Arlington. Texas' top attraction, Six Flags has drawn more than 50 million visitors from around the world since it opened its doors in 1961. Situated 20 minutes from both downtown Dallas and Fort Worth, the park offers more than 100 rides, shows, and attractions on its 205 acres. The six flags flying above the entrance commemorate the days when Texas was under the countries of Spain, France, and Mexico, when it was a Republic, when it briefly was part of the Confederacy, and now as a state in the United States. A separate part of the park is devoted to each flag.

DALLAS AND FORT WORTH 71

Some of the more celebrated attractions include: the $2.1 million Cliffhanger—the first total freefall ride gives riders the sensation of stepping off the top of a 9-story building; the Texas Chute Out, a 200-ft. parachute drop; Judge Roy Scream, the huge wooden roller coaster; the Shock Wave, the longest, tallest, fastest double-loop roller coaster anywhere; the 300-ft. high oil derrick, with views, from the top, of both downtown skylines, the log flume and the Roaring Rapids river ride, where passengers are guaranteed to cool off, the narrow-gauge railroad encircling the park and Air Racer—biplanes circling a 14-story tower.

The park is always undergoing improvements and additions. One of the latest is the Silver Star Carousel. This fully restored 1926 carousel is an example of more than 30,000 man-hours of painstaking restoration.

The Southern Palace features full-scale musical revues with 5 hours of shows throughout the day. During selected summer nights, the park features shows in the 10,000-seat Music Mill Amphitheater, top-name entertainment in concert. Six Flags pioneered the one-price ticket: At this writing, $17.95 for adults, $11.95 for children under 48 inches tall, and free for children age 2 or younger. Two-consecutive-day tickets are available for $22.95. The park is open weekends in the spring and fall, with daily operation in the summer (the park opens at 10 A.M.; closing times vary widely). Call ahead (214) 640–8900, ext. 517.

Wet 'n Wild. Just across the street from Six Flags, one of the newest additions to the Dallas-Fort Worth theme-park crowd is a (somewhat enlarged) copy of another Wet'n Wild in Orlando, Florida. The 47-acre park offers its visitors the chance to splash, slide, ride, float, paddle, dive, and, if you look sharp, swim.

Fifteen rides are offered, among them the Kamikaze Waterslide (a six-story, 300-foot long slip down into a pool), the Banzai Boggan (a watery roller coaster), the Corkscrew Flume, and, for the more leisurely minded, the Lazy River and the River Raft Ride.

There's food on sale—the usual poolside snacks (hamburgers, hot dogs, pizza, etc.)—and picnic areas, if you want to enjoy your meal on solid ground.

The park is open for weekends only in May and September, 10 A.M. to 6 P.M. During June, July, and August, it's open all week, 10 A.M. to 9P.M. (10 P.M. weekends). Admission is $13.86 for adults, $11.72 for kids 3–12, $6.90 for seniors. Under 2 swim free. Parking is free, and there's shuttle-bus service to and from the park from many of the area hotels. (817) 265–3356. A second Wet 'n Wild can be found at 12715 LBJ Freeway, Garland; (214) 271–5637. Admission to the 22-acre park is comparable to the larger Wet 'n Wild and the park is open weekends in May and for part of September. Early hours are 10 A.M.–6 P.M. for half of June and half of September. From mid-June to September the park is open till 9. Ten rides are available.

River Ridge Pavilion. 3201 Riverfront, Fort Worth; 817–335–7472. Open 10 A.M.–7 P.M. daily during the spring and summer. No admission charge; rental fees. River Ridge Pavilion is open to the public for putt putt golf, shuffleboard, Ping-Pong, boating (paddle boats and canoes), and cycling. There also is roller skating along the paths that meander along the river. Snack bar available nearby.

The Fishin' Place. 6401 South Stemmons, south of Denton; (817) 497–3837. Open weekdays from 8 A.M. till dark, 7 A.M. on weekends. Call for winter times (they vary daily). Admission: $1.65 per person; children under seven are free. Let the kids "go fish" at this stocked fishing hole/park north of Dallas. The fishing is out of two large ponds that contain catfish. Cane poles can be rented ($1). You can buy bait at the Fishin' Place or bring it from home. In addition to the admission charge, fishers are charged $2 a pound for fish caught. You can have the fish cleaned for an additional charge.

Wax Museum of the Southwest. 601 E. Safari Parkway (I-30 at Belt Line), in Grand Prairie. Over 300 famous personalities are depicted in over 100 wax scenes in this museum, the largest of its kind in the Southwest. Displays include the gun battle at the O.K. Corral, Bonnie and Clyde, President John F. Kennedy, and the life and Last Supper of Jesus Christ. Also on display are collections of rare antique guns and weapons, barbed wire, pre-Columbian art, Indian artifacts, Western art, and restored examples of early transportation. The museum is home for the American Cattle Breeders Hall of Fame, a tribute to some of America's best cattle and cattle breeders. Open daily year-round (except New Year's Day, Thanksgiving, and Christmas). Hours are: Memorial Day to Labor Day, 10 A.M. to 9 P.M.; the rest of the year, Monday through Friday, 10 A.M. to 5 P.M.; and Saturday and Sunday till 6 P.M. The box office closes 1 hour before scheduled closing. Adults $6.37, ages 4 to 12 $5.31. Call (214) 263-2391 for information.

International Wildlife Park. 601 Wildlife Parkway (off I-30 and Belt Line), in Grand Prairie. Featuring one of the best collections of exotic wildlife in the country, this drive-through park is home to more than 2,000 animals, including rhinos, hippos, zebras, giraffes, elephants, ostriches, camels, and cape buffalo. They can be viewed roaming freely in their natural settings as visitors drive their own automobiles, windows down, through the animal preserve. Most visitors allow 1½ to 2 hours to meander along the paved roads within the 350-acre park. The Entertainment Village features a children's petting zoo, boat rides, and special animal shows and exhibits including elephant rides. All rides, shows, and attractions are included in the single admission price. The park is open daily, Memorial Day to Labor Day, 9:30 A.M. to 6:30 P.M., (last car admitted), and weekends only in October and November. Admission is $9.95 for 7–adult, $7.45 for 3–6, and free under 2. For just the drive-through, the fee is $6.95. For information on special group discounts, call (214) 265-2203.

Malibu Grand Prix of Dallas, 11150 Malibu (620–7575) and **Malibu Grand Prix,** 609 N.E. Loop 820, Hurst (589–0523). Racing buffs drive scaled-down race cars around ½ mile track at these two locations. Open from around noon till 10 P.M. or midnight nightly. Must be at least 8 years old to drive. Separate sessions for children and adults. Cost about $2. Affiliated with these two, there is a miniature golf facility with bumper boats, batting cages, and arcade games at 11130 Malibu, open daily, 10 A.M.–1 A.M.; no admission fee.

State Fair Park. 2 mi. east of downtown via I-30. The Midway is open daily the two and a half weeks of the State Fair of Texas in October, and weekends April through Labor Day. Tickets must be purchased for the rides, but admission to grounds and picnic areas is free when the fair is not in session. (See the *Parks* section, above.)

Open in summer, **Sandy Lake Park,** 1800 Sandy Lake Rd., Carrollton; 242-7449. Family-owned amusement park featuring rides, swimming, golf, paddle boats. End of March 10 A.M.–6 P.M. weekends through end of May, then open daily till 8 P.M. to September. Admission $1.50, under 4 free.

RANCH EXPERIENCES. Dallas and Tarrant Counties represent the largest concentration of horses—some 65,000—in the nation. At this writing there are more than 20 stables and horseback-riding facilities in the Metroplex open to the public. Check the Yellow Pages of either city for the stables closest to your day's activities.

From Fort Worth's revitalized Stockyards to rodeos (see the *Spectator Sports* section, below) from Mansfield to Mesquite, the visitor to Dallas-Fort Worth area chasing his image of the West and its cowboys will not be *too* disappointed.

The **West Fork Ranch** at Fort Worth is operated by the Murrin Bros. Land and Cattle Co. For information or reservations, write them at Stockyards Station, P.O. Box 4130, Fort Worth, TX 76106, or call (817) 624-1101.

The **Kowbell Ranch** has a bull-riding event Monday and Friday year-round; $3 for adults, $2 for kids under 12. There's also a rodeo every Saturday and Sunday for $5 and $2.50, respectively. The ranch is southeast of Fort Worth north of intersection of Texas 157 and Business 287, Texas 157, 8 mi. south of I-20. For information call (214) 477-3092.

CHILDREN'S ACTIVITIES. Vast layouts such as *Six Flags Over Texas,* and *International Wildlife Park,* to name just a few in the area (See *Theme Parks and Amusement Centers,* just above), can keep a child content from sunup to sundown—if he lasts that long. If the pocketbook calls for activities on the lighter, sometimes quieter side, both Dallas and Fort Worth offer good to excellent zoological parks, each for $2 or less. The *Fort Worth Zoological Park* is the starting point for the 5-mi. *Forest Park Train,* the world's longest miniature-train ride (90¢). The *Fort Worth Museum of Science and History,* offering natural-history displays and a planetarium, is the largest educational museum for children in the country features a mammoth Omni-Max theater (projection with a 360-degree view); $4.75 for adults, $3.00 children under 12. Call 732-1631 for information. The area proffers an array of miniature golf courses, go-kart tracks, coin-operated game arcades, city swimming pools (summers only) and smaller amusement parks, such as *Penny Whistle Park,* 10717 E. Northwest Highway at Plano Road; (214) 348-8297. Check the Yellow Pages of both Dallas and Fort Worth for locations closest to your "headquarters." (Also, see the *Parks, Zoos,* and *Museums* sections here.)

LAKES. Texas boasts a total of 6,300 sq. mi. of lakes and streams, surpassed only by Alaska. Interestingly enough, Caddo Lake, on the Louisiana line, is the only large natural lake. The Lakes Trail, one of 10 state-designated Travel Trails guiding motorists to major points of scenic, historical, and recreational interest throughout much of Texas, practically encircles the Dallas-Fort Worth North Texas area. As on other trails, the route generally avoids crowded freeways and interstates. Folders are available from the Texas tourist bureaus (the closest to Dallas-Fort Worth are Denison on U.S. 75/69 and Gainesville on U.S. 71/I-35) or by writing the State Department of Highways and Public Transportation (see *Facts at Your Fingertips* at the front of this book). Fort Worth and Tarrant

County have the most lakes of any city and county in Texas; they are: Eagle Mountain, Benbrook, Lake Worth, Grapevine, Arlington, and Joe Pool.

There are numerous lakes in the surrounding communities and countrysides, most with facilities for swimming, boating, fishing, camping, and picnicking. Check the Thursday sports sections of the *Dallas Morning News, Dallas Times Herald,* and *Fort Worth Star-Telegram* for up-to-date fishing reports on North and East Texas lakes. Fishing licenses are available at sporting-goods stores. For current information about area lakes, call (214) 670–4100 or (817) 334–2150. Most amenities are available at cost.

Following is an alphabetical offering. (Some facts and figures courtesy of the Texas Highway Department, Travel and Information Division.)

Lake Arlington. 2,275 acres in southwest Arlington off Loop 303. Owned and operated by the city. Popular for boating, sailing, and waterskiing. Facilities for boaters and fishermen. White and black bass. Municipal and commercial parks.

Bachman Lake. Small lake in northwest Dallas on Northwest Highway (Loop 12) near Love Field. Popular for afternoon or weekend picnics, jogging, bicycling, roller-skating. Paddle boats for rent. No waterskiing. Near a restaurant-and-nightclub strip.

Lake Benbrook. 3,770 acres 10 mi. southwest of Fort Worth in Benbrook on Lake Shore Drive off U.S. 377. A Corps of Engineers impoundment on the clear fork of the Trinity River. Lakeside parks with picnic facilities, camping and trailer areas, restrooms, drinking water, launching ramps, fishing supplies, snack bar. Waterskiing, horseback riding, swimming, golf. Fees for some areas. Call 292–2400 for information.

Eagle Mountain Lake. 8,500 acres 12 mi. northwest of Fort Worth on west fork of Trinity River. All water sports. Trailer areas, restrooms, snack bars, boat rentals, launching ramps, fishing supplies. Fishing good year-round, with schooling white bass in spring.

Lake Granbury. 8,500 acres at De Cordova Bend on the Brazos River. 103-mi. shoreline. Parks, camps, service facilities.

Lake Grapevine. 7,380 acres 25 mi. northeast of downtown Fort Worth, 25 mi. northwest of downtown Dallas near the city of Grapevine. A Corps of Engineers reservoir. 60-mi. shoreline. Campsites, picnic areas, boat ramps, marina service, swimming, fishing supplies, boat rentals, golf. Call 481–4541 for information.

Joe Pool. 30,600 acres about 7 miles southwest of Dallas, south of Grand Prairie. Camping, picknicking, launching ramps, swimming, waterskiing. 6 parks on the lake.

Lake Lavon. 22,000 acres about 10 mi. north of Rockwell. A Corps of Engineers reservoir. Four parks with hookups for campers. Day-use parks, motorcycle trail, park (Caddo) especially for the disabled. Boat ramps, marina services, swimming beaches, duck hunting in specified area.

Lake Lewisville. 23,280 acres about 25 mi. north of downtown Dallas off I-35E. Formerly called the Garza-Little Elm Reservoir. A Corps of Engineers reservoir. Popular with area residents for water sports. A dozen public parks. Marinas, boat rentals, launching ramps, fishing, supplies, swimming, waterskiing, sailing, camping, trailer and picnic areas.

Mountain Creek Lake. 2,940 acres in southwest Dallas near the Dallas naval air station and Grand Prairie. Popular for fishing, boating.

DALLAS AND FORT WORTH

Lake Ray Hubbard. 22,745 acres 10 mi. east of Dallas on east fork of the Trinity River. Owned by city of Dallas for municipal water supply and recreation. Lakeside marinas, camps, housing developments. Excellent fishing and boating.

White Rock Lake. Scenic lake in northeast Dallas, accessible off Garland Road (Texas 78) and Northwest Highway (Loop 12). Popular for sailing and fishing. Lakeside picnic and park facilities. No waterskiing. (See also the *Parks* section, above.)

Lake Worth. 3,247 acres 9 mi. northwest of Fort Worth on Texas 199, also accessible from Loop 820. Scenic vistas along Meandering Drive. Popular for boating, waterskiing, sailing. Parks and picnic areas. (See also the "Fort Worth Nature Center" entry in the *Parks* section, above.)

Some of the lakes worth a 90-minute drive from Dallas-Fort Worth include

Lake Texoma. 89,000 acres on the Texas-Oklahoma line on the Red River. One of the largest reservoirs in Texas. Shoreline of 580 miles. Scenic coves and inlets. This popular Corps of Engineers lake draws more than 9 million visitors a year. 57 modern campgrounds, scores of trailer parks, 110 picnic areas, 100 shelter buildings, 80 boat ramps. Marinas and luxury resorts. All types of boating activity. Some of best fishing in the nation: black bass, crappie, white bass, plus lunker catfish. Information available at south end of the dam on U.S. 75A.

Lake Tawakoni. 36,700 acres east of Dallas. Sabine River Authority reservoir. 200-mi. shoreline spreads over three counties. Marinas, camps, parks on wooded shores. Boat ramps, designated water-ski areas. Good fishing in countless coves and inlets. More than 5 sq. mi. of submerged-timber prime habitat. Information at north end of Iron Bridge Dam off FM 47 south of Point, Texas.

Cedar Creek Lake. 33,750 acres southeast of Dallas. This popular North-Central Texas recreation area supplies Fort Worth's water. Amid post oaks and pines. Campsites, picnicking areas, excellent fishing, swimming, boating.

Lake Whitney. 15,760 acres on Brazos River south of Fort Worth. A Corps of Engineers impoundment. More than 4 million visitors a year. Numerous campsites, marinas, parks, recreation areas, housing developments. Fishing good in sheltered coves and inlet. Depths ranging to 100 ft.; popular with scuba divers. State Park on its eastern edge.

Possum Kingdom Lake. 19,800 acres west of Fort Worth. Lakeside resorts and camps. Favorite with swimmers, scuba divers, boaters, fishermen. Woodlands surround lake. State Park on the southwestern shore.

CAMPING. The 106-acre Texas "flea market" called **Traders Village**, at 2602 Mayfield Road in Grand Prairie, includes a recreational-vehicle park open every day of the year. For more information on availability of the 200 hookups, call (214) 647–8205. You'll never be lonely here on the weekends, when everything imaginable is bought and sold Saturday and Sunday from 8 A.M. to dusk. Hundreds of booths and stalls feature collectible treasures, and craftsmen show off their skills and wares. The village also houses an antique carousel, children's ride, a restaurant, and concession stands. Among the many special events during the year is the Prairie

Dog Chili Cook Off & Pickled Quail Egg World Championship. For information and selling space at Traders Village call (214) 647-2331.

Arlington KOA. Midway between Dallas and Fort Worth, just off I-20 (exit 449, 1½ miles north on Hwy. 157). 150 sites and trailer storage. Swimming pool, recreation room, other facilities. In Mid-Cities area near Six Flags, etc. (817) 461-0101.

See also the *Lakes* and *State Parks* sections here.

STATE PARKS. One of the best sources of information on Texas' state parks can be found in a folder, appropriately titled *Texas State Park Information,* available from Texas tourist bureaus (the closest to Dallas-Fort Worth are Denison on U.S. 75/69 and Gainesville on U.S. 77/I-35) or by writing the Texas Parks and Wildlife Department, 4200 Smith School Road, Austin, TX 78744.

The parks department maintains some 101 state parks as scenic attractions, recreational areas, and historic sites. No hunting of any kind is permitted, although fishing is, and boats, fishing licenses, and supplies are normally available. The folder breaks down each state park as to the availability of camping, screened shelters, group facilities, campsites with electricity and sewage, campsites with water and electricity, rest rooms, showers, cabins, picnicking, groceries, fishing, swimming, waterskiing, boat ramp, museum/exhibit, historic structure, day-use only, group trailer, trailer dump station, nature trail, and miscellaneous.

Some of the state parks in the Dallas-Fort Worth area are: **Acton,** burial site of Davy Crockett's wife, near Granbury; **Bonham,** home of Sam Rayburn; **Cleburne; Dinosaur Valley,** near Glen Rose; **Eisenhower** and **Eisenhower Birthplace,** at Denison; **Fort Richardson,** at Jacksboro; **Governor Hogg Shrine** at Quitman; **Lake Mineral Wells; Lake Whitney; Possum Kingdom** near the town of Caddo, and **Tyler.**

With a state park on its eastern edge, **Lake Whitney** (15,760 acres on the Brazos River near Hillsboro) draws more than 3 million visitors a year to its campsites, marinas, parks, and recreation areas. Fishing is reported excellent in sheltered coves and inlets. Depths ranging to 100 feet are popular with scuba divers.

Woodland-surrounded **Possum Kingdom Lake** (19,800 acres west of Fort Worth) attracts its share of scuba divers, too. Lakeside resorts and camps are favorites with swimmers, boaters, and fishermen alike. The state park is on the lake's southwestern shore.

PARTICIPANT SPORTS. As evidenced by its growth, Dallas-Fort Worth does not sit still for long periods. Neither do many of the sports-minded residents, and visitors to the area can benefit from the expansive offering of facilities—in addition to the hot-summer and mild-winter conditions. People in great numbers can be seen fishing (see the *Lakes* section) and playing golf, tennis, softball, and racquetball. They run (the White Rock Marathon, Cowtown Marathon, and Turkey Trot are here), jog (witness Dr. Kenneth Cooper's famous Aerobics Center), and go boating, sailing, waterskiing, and wind surfing. They ice skate, roller-skate, ride horses, cycle, bowl, take in local gun ranges, and sweat it out in numerous health clubs. And they can be seen soaking up the sun at White Rock and Bachman Lakes on either end of Northwest Highway in Dallas, at Trinity and Forest Parks in Fort Worth, and at area swimming pools and lakes.

Public golf courses in Dallas include: *Tenison,* 3501 Samuell Blvd., 670–1402, *Stevens Park,* 1005 N. Montclair, 670–7506, *Cedar Crest Golf Course,* 1800 Southerland, 670–7615, and *L. B. Houston,* 11223 Luna Rd., 670–6322.

Fort Worth has: *Meadowbrook,* 1815 Jensen Rd., 456–4616; *Pecan Valley,* Benbrook Lake, 249–1845; *Rockwood,* 1851 Jacksboro Hwy., 624–1771; *Sycamore Creek,* 2423 E. Vickery, 535–7241, and *Z. Boaz,* 3240 Lackland Rd., 738–6287. *Grapevine,* below Grapevine Dam, is rated highly among the many courses.

Tennis. With 22 outdoor and five indoor courts, Fort Worth's *Mary Potishman Lard Tennis Center* (3609 Bellaire Dr. N. on the TCU campus; 921–7960 or 921–7808) is open daily. The *McLeland Tennis Center* (1600 W. Seminary; 921–5134), with 16 outdoor courts, is open Monday to Friday, 9 A.M. to 10 P.M., and Saturday and Sunday, 9 A.M. to 9 P.M. To reserve any of 200 Dallas city-park tennis courts, call 428–1501 between 8:15 A.M. and 5:15 P.M. no more than a day ahead of time.

At this writing there are more than 20 stables and **horseback-riding** facilities in the Metroplex open to the public. Check the Yellow Pages of either city for the ones closest to your activities. **Ice skating** is available at Prestonwood Town Center (Dallas Parkway at Belt Line) and the Galleria (Dallas Parkway and Loop 635), both in Far North Dallas; Plaza of the Americas in downtown Dallas, and Tandy Center in downtown Fort Worth.

Popular **bike** paths in Dallas are found at: Bachman Lake, 3.08 mi., 3500 W. Northwest Hwy.; White Rock Lake, 11.1 mi., 8300 Garland Rd.; White White Rock Creek Trail, 7.1 mi., Mockingbird and W. Lather to Hillcrest and Valley View; 8300 Garland Rd.; Crawford Park, 2 mi., 8700 Elam Rd.; Kiest Park, 3 mi., 3000 S. Hampton Rd.; Netherland Park, ¼ mi., 5700 Meaders La. at Netherland, and Singing Hills Park, ½ mi., 1010 Crough Rd. For information or maps, call 670–4027. Fort Worth has bike paths through the scenic Forest Park area, along the Trinity River.

SPECTATOR SPORTS. Dallas-Fort Worth takes no off season from sports. The hottest ticket in town, the Dallas Cowboys of the National **Football** League, light up Texas Stadium in Irving from August exhibition games through, in most seasons, January's playoffs. The Texas Rangers of the American League West invade the **baseball** diamond at Arlington Stadium on the old Dallas-Fort Worth Turnpike (I-30) from April through early October. Shuttle-bus service is available to both stadiums; contact team offices (Cowboys, 214–429–1181; Rangers, 817–273–5100) for more information.

The Dallas Mavericks of the National **Basketball** Association play from early autumn to late spring at Dallas's downtown Reunion Arena (658–7070), also site of the WCT Finals in April or May. The Willow Bend **Polo** and Hunt Club in Plano (call 214–248–6298 for schedule) opens some of its matches to the public.

The Mesquite Championship **Rodeo,** (214) 285–8777, at I-635 and Military Parkway in Mesquite, kicks every Friday and Saturday night from April through September. Fort Worth's Cowtown Rodeo, (817) 624–1101, May through October (performances every Friday night) and from the last weekend in September (during Pioneer Days) through mid-November. Its arena, the historic Cowtown Coliseum in the Stockyards area, opened its doors to the public in 1908 and staged the world's first indoor contest rodeo in 1917. In Mansfield, southeast of Fort Worth, the KowBell Rodeo (214) 477–3092 is the country's only year-round indoor rodeo, with performances every Saturday night. The group of buildings that make up the Will Rogers Memorial Center and its new Equestrian Center in Fort Worth plays host, at various times of the year, to horse shows, boxing and wrestling matches, rodeos and auto shows, in addition to other community events. Rodeos also are a big attraction at the Southwestern Exposition, Fat Stock Show, and Rodeo in Fort Worth in late January and early February.

Wrestling is on tap every Friday night at the Sportatorium (565–9261) in Dallas and every Monday night at Will Rogers Coliseum. Weekend **auto races** are staged at various tracks throughout the Metroplex, from Kennedale to North Richland Hills, Mansfield, Grand Prairie, Carrollton, and Mesquite.

In addition to other college-sports programs, several universities compete on the **college gridiron,** including the Southern Methodist Mustangs and Bishop College Tigers in Dallas, Texas Christian University Horned Frogs in Fort Worth, University of Texas at Arlington Mavericks, North Texas Mean Green in Denton, and Austin College Kangaroos in Sherman. The annual clash between the University of Texas at Austin and the University of Oklahoma is staged in the Cotton Bowl the second Saturday in October. The Cotton Bowl Classic, usually staged New Year's Day in Dallas, pits the Southwest Conference football champion against another highly ranked team at State Fair Park.

The Quaker State Open in Grand Prairie in February hosts the professional **bowlers'** tour. The Virginia Slims women's **tennis** circuit comes to Dallas (Moody Coliseum) in March, followed by the men's World Championship Tennis Finals (Reunion Arena) in late April or early May. The Metroplex enjoys two stops on the Professional **Golfers** Association tour, the Byron Nelson Classic at Las Colinas in Irving, and the National Invitation Tournament at Colonial Country Club in Fort Worth.

A tour of **Texas Stadium,** home of the Dallas Cowboys and the SMU Mustangs, is available at the Irving facility Monday through Friday, 10 A.M. and 2 P.M., and Saturdays, Sundays, and holidays, 11 A.M., 12:30 P.M., and 2 P.M. (no tours on games days). The tour begins between gates 10 and 1 and includes the press box, Stadium Club, playing field, locker room, and gift shop. Adults, $4; children under 12, $2. Getting into the stadium can be tricky: Take I-35 north from downtown, exit left to Texas 183, take the Loop 12 North exit, then pull into the stadium's gate-1 parking lot. Call Texas Stadium, (214) 438–7676, for information. Free parking.

HISTORIC SITES. FORT WORTH. The **Fort Worth Stockyards** area, North Main and Exchange Ave., retains the flavor of the Old West many visitors come to Fort Worth to see. But make no mistake, the revitalized North Side is real; it just has a few new coats of paint, an attractive river walk, and now the world's largest honkytonk. This is Cowtown, complete with restaurants, saloons, art galleries, western-wear stores, and special shops selling apparel and merchandise of the historic cattle era. There are even a bootmaker and a tattoo parlor. The Stockyards and Cattlemen's Exchange conducts livestock auctions on Mondays, and working cowboys put on rodeos at the Cowtown Coliseum, scene of the world's first indoor rodeo.

Surrounded by a 14-square-block City Center project that includes the Worthington Hotel and two tall towers, **Sundance Square,** at Main and Houston, Fort Worth, has returned a portion of downtown Fort Worth to the turn of the century. The restoration—with restaurants, specialty shops, art galleries, a western-art museum, and other businesses accented by bricked sidewalks, landscaping, and period-style lampposts—is named for Butch Cassidy and the Sundance Kid, who used the city's Hell's Half Acre as their hideout around 1900.

Restored **Thistle Hill,** 1509 Pennsylvania Ave. at Summit, is the last remaining mansion of the rich cattle barons. Open Monday through Friday, with tours hourly 10 A.M. to 3 P.M. and Sunday, 1 to 4 P.M. (closed Saturday). Admission is $2. For more information call (817) 336–1212.

The **Will Rogers Statue** in front of the Will Rogers Memorial Center (3400 W. Lancaster, Fort Worth) depicts the legendary humorist and actor astride his horse Soap Suds.

The Fort Worth Park and Recreation Department's collection of seven architecturally and historically significant Texas log structures dating from 1850 to 1860 makes up the **Log Cabin Village Historical Complex** at the corner of Log Cabin Village Lane and University Drive. Men and women dressed in costumes demonstrate pioneer crafts and produce for sale, in the gift shop, stone-ground cornmeal from the grist mill, hand-dipped candles, handwoven material, quilts, and corn-shuck dolls. The 7.6-acre location is in tree-shaded Forest Park at the corner of University Dr. and Log Cabin Village La. The village is open Monday through Friday, 8 A.M. to 4:30 P.M. (except Thanksgiving, Christmas, and New Year's Day); Sat. 11 to 4:30 P.M., Sun. 1 to 4:30 P.M. Adults, $1; children, 50¢. For information call (817) 926–5881. Nearby, **Van Zandt Cottage** (Lancaster at University Dr.) was once used as a stopping place by both stagecoach passengers and cattlemen. It now is restored and furnished with antiques of the same period.

DALLAS. Chosen as the relocation site for endangered historical structures by the Dallas County Heritage Society, **Old City Park,** 1717 Gano St. at St. Paul, is a 13-acre "museum" of architectural and cultural history juxtaposed against the skyline of Dallas. Life in North Central Texas between 1840 and 1910 is depicted in: Millermore, the largest remaining antebellum home in North Central Texas, plus a railroad depot, a general store, blacksmith shop, a pottery kiln, a doctor's office, a smoke house, a merchandise store, and nearly 25 other period structures. Brent Place Restaurant, (214) 421–3057, is open for lunch, and a gift shop sells old-timey objects. Also on the grounds are a church and a bandstand, popular settings for weddings; rest rooms; and a popcorn vendor. The grounds are staffed by volunteers and open free, sunup to sundown. A fee is charged to tour the museum buildings (adults, $4; senior citizens, $2; children 6 to 12, $2), Tuesday through Saturday, 10 A.M. to 4 P.M., and Sunday, 1:30 to 4:30 P.M. (closed Monday). The park location was first a buffalo trace, then an Indian campground. Call (214) 421–7800 for information.

Downtown Dallas's historical plaza—bounded by Elm, Market, Commerce, and Record Sts.—features two markedly different structures. The **John Neely Bryan cabin** (1841), substantiated as the residence of the first

Dallasite, was made of handhewn logs chinked with clay. It also served as Dallas's first courthouse in the 1850s.

A note for photographers: You can dramatize the contrast of old and new in Dallas by snapping a photograph of the Bryan cabin, "Old Red" stone courthouse, and futuristic Reunion Tower—all in the same frame. Stand on the north side of Elm Street and look southwestward.

Across Main Street from the Bryan cabin in the **John F. Kennedy Memorial Plaza,** some 200 yards from where the president was assassinated on Nov. 22, 1963, stands a 30-ft. white cenotaph designed by Philip Johnson. Rarely a day goes by that tourists don't congregate here to reflect—and, in **Dealey Plaza,** two blocks to the west on Houston Street, to stare up at what was then called the Texas Schoolbook Depository Building on Elm, whence the fatal shots are said to have been fired.

Just north of here begins the **West End Historic District,** bounded by Woodall Rodgers, Elm, Record, and Lamar streets. This area of warehouses, some dating to the early 1900s, has undergone a revitalization and successfully drawn companies and people back to the area. Trendy restaurants and night spots continue to open. The nearby renovated Brewery complex offers still more chic eateries and bars. Among other West-End historical structures is **Union Station** (1916), restored to its original beauxarts style of Texas architecture. It houses Amtrak passenger service, a visitor information center, and, upstairs in the Grand Hall, a restaurant complex. While in the area, visitors should rise above it all via a glass elevator to the observation deck 50 stories up in the geodesic dome of **Reunion Tower.**

After years of neglect, portions of **Oak Cliff,** more than 100 square miles of south Dallas real estate, are being restored. Beautiful hills, bluffs, and tree-lined streets were the setting, between 1890 and 1930, for distinguished homes of Dallas's socialites and politicians. Efforts are being made to preserve existing neighborhoods, such as in the Winnetka Heights Historic District and its 850 homes bounded by Davis, 12th, Polk, and Rosemont. Today, Oak Cliff is home to 100 parks (including the zoo), 40 city pools and sports fields, two municipal golf courses, two country clubs, an airport, and three colleges (Bishop, Dallas Baptist, and Mountain View).

Listed in the *National Register of Historic Places,* **Swiss Avenue** is a historic neighborhood of homes just east of downtown Dallas. Tours of homes are held in September.

DeGolyer Estate. 8525 Garland Rd., also listed the *National Register of Historic Places,* comprises 44 acres on the shores of White Rock Lake in East Dallas. Filled with English and Spanish antiques, the mansion is open for guided tours and is housed in the Dallas Arboretum and Botanic Gardens. The estate hosts a variety of cultural and educational programs during the year, in addition to free concerts in the formal gardens. Call (214) 327-8263.

Available at the Visitors Information Center in Union Station, 400 S. Houston St. in downtown Dallas, *A Guide for Seeing Dallas County History* is invaluable to the history buff chasing the Dallas of yesteryear and was compiled by the Dallas Historical Commission and Heritage Trails Map Committee. It is also available at D.B. McCall's stores in Old City Park, West End Marketplace, and NorthPark Shopping Mall, and at the Arboretum and the Dallas Historical Commission offices.

LIBRARIES. Every major city has a library, even a system of them. And most visitors usually don't need—or want—to be pushed in the direction of one. They can get their fill of books and bindings at home, thank you. But oh, Bennett Cerf, if you could see Dallas now! The famous publisher once described the Dallas Public Library, recently renamed the J. Erik Jonsson Central Library, as the world's worst. But he died in 1971, barely a year after plans began to build a new central facility.

In the spring of 1982, one of the most modern libraries in the nation opened to the tune of $43 million in downtown Dallas across from City Hall. The new library at 1515 Young St.; (670-140), which replaces the Commerce Street location, houses 2.3 million volumes (over and above the capacities of branch facilities) and accommodates some 1,300 readers in reading nooks and balconies. Visitors are quickly impressed with the cable-TV studio, computers, theater, exhibit hall, listening rooms, library store, and snack bar.

Though it's *only* the seventh-largest city in the nation, Dallas has a library system that in terms of the number of books available for residents ranks 14th among the largest cities in the country.

MUSEUMS. For a city its size, Fort Worth has an exceptional complex of four major museums—three art, one science and history. This cultural district, within a four-square-block area less than 2 mi. west of downtown, has been rightly called the Acropolis of the Southwest. All buildings are within easy walking distance, accessible to the disabled, and open free, in most cases, to the public. Dallas has fine museums too, the largest group of them being within State Fair Park, 2 mi. east of downtown.

Dallas

The Dallas Museum of Art, formerly the Museum of Fine Arts, moved in early 1984 from State Fair Park to its new Edward Larrabee Barnes-designed building in the new Arts District, in northeast downtown at 1717 N. Harwood in late October 1983. The new museum is the result of one of the largest capital campaigns ever organized in the city. The drive gained wide public awareness several years ago during a major traveling exhibit, Pompeii AD 79. Voters later approved $25 million in bonds for the new building, to be matched by $15 million in private donations. Actual donations totaled $27.6 million. and $25 million in new art was pledged from private collections. The museum facade is of huge blocks of Indiana limestone.

The permanent collection of 19th- and 20th-century American and European, pre-Columbian, African, classical, Impressionist, and Oriental works, and a new Decorative Arts Wing, is bolstered by 10 to 12 temporary exhibitions each year. Featured in the permanent collection are works by Matisse, Gauguin, Wyeth, Courbet, and Picasso. Facilities include an extensive art library, a restaurant, a sculpture garden, and a children's gallery. Open Tuesday through Saturday, 10 to 5 P.M. (Thursday till 9 P.M.), and Sunday from noon to 5. Free. Call (214) 922-0220.

Dallas's largest concentration of museums is within State Fair Park, 2 mi. east of downtown.

The Dallas Museum of Natural History, at the entrance to the park, presents 54 natural habitats authentically re-created and furnished with actual specimens including a 90-million-year-old fossil fish, and the Close-ups Room allows visitors to handle and inspect changing specimens. The museum also sponsors periodic environmental exhibits, lectures, and field trips. Open Monday through Saturday, 9 A.M. to 5 P.M., and Sunday, from noon to 5 P.M. Free. Call 670–8457.

Since its founding in 1946, what is now called **The Science Place Two,** housed in a smaller and older building than that of Science Place One, has become an outstanding resource center and educational showcase. Major traveling exhibits have included the record-breaking Ice Age Art exhibit, the Dreamstage exhibit—a portrait of the sleeping brain—and China: 2000 Years of Discovery. Permanent exhibits expound on the human anatomy and health, as well as electronics, banking, and transportation. The first solar-powered airplane is here as is a planetarium. Open Tuesday through Saturday, 9:30 A.M. to 5:30 P.M., and Sunday, from noon to 5:30 P.M. $1 adult, 50¢ child. Planetarium shows at scheduled times ($1). 428–7200. The main phone number is 428–8351. **Science Place One** is a "hands-on" museum featuring a gallery housing the Goodwin Seashell Collection; "Looking at the Lights," an interactive exhibit on the nature of light; and will house "A Kid's Place" geared for 2–8-year-olds. Fee is $3 for adults and $2 for 7–16-year-olds.

The Age of Steam Railroad Museum, a venture of the Southwest Railroad Historical Society and the State Fair of Texas, represents a collection of historical freight and passenger cars and engines from 1900 to 1950. A collection of railroad locomotives is on a siding of the Missouri-Pacific track adjacent. Open 10 A.M.–6 P.M. daily during the State Fair in October; other times at 9 A.M.–1 P.M. Thursday and Friday, 11 A.M.–5 P.M. Saturday and Sunday. Adults $2, children under 16 years $1, 421–8754.

The Dallas Aquarium features 340 species of amphibians, reptiles, and native freshwater, tropical and cold-water fish. Feeding times open to the public are: Monday through Friday 9 A.M.–11 A.M. Open Monday through Saturday, 9 A.M. to 5 P.M., and Sunday from noon. Free. Call 670–8441.

The Art Deco **Hall of State,** in the center of the park, was created to honor the Texas Centennial of 1936. It tells the story of Texas and Dallas through thousands of historical objects and costumes, documents, and photographs. The hall also features a series of temporary exhibitions and has a growing publications program. Open Monday through Saturday, 9 A.M. to 5 P.M., and Sunday, 1 to 5 P.M. (The lower floor houses the Dallas Historical Society Research Center.) Free. 421–5136.

A turn-of-the-century fire station, **Old Tige's Dallas Firefighters Museum,** at 3801 Parry Ave., features an 1884 horse-drawn steam pumper and antique alarm bells. Call 821–1500. Free, but donations are accepted.

The Biblical Arts Center, at 7500 Park La. at Boedeker near NorthPark Center in North Dallas, features early-Christian architecture and biblical and secular art. The 30-minute light-and-sound biblical presentation, made several times daily, includes the unveiling of the 124-by-20-foot oil painting *The Miracle at Pentecost.* Shows start at half-past the hour, with the last presentation beginning at 4:30 P.M. Open Tuesday through Saturday 10 A.M. to 5 P.M., and Sunday, from 1 P.M. Adults $3.75, ages 6–12 $2, and under 6 free. Call 691–4661.

Currently housed on the campus of Bishop College in Oak Cliff, the **Museum of African-American Art and Culture** is the only center of its kind in the Southwest, recognizing the contributions of black Americans.

Founded in 1974, the museum (3837 Simpson-Stuart) offers a collection of modern and traditional works, as well as traveling exhibitions and musical performances, and should be featured in State Park sometime in 1990. Free. Call 372-5222.

The International Museum of Culture, 7500 W. Camp Wisdom Road, Dallas; (214) 709-2406 focuses on contemporary cultures of the world, with dioramas, displays, and audio-visual shows. Tues.-Fri. 10 A.M. to 5 P.M.; Sat. and Sun., 1:30 P.M. Closed Mon. Free.

Fort Worth

Amon Carter Museum, at 3501 Camp Bowie (738-1933) owes its beginnings to its namesake, the prominent Fort Worther. First introduced to the painting and sculpture of Charles M. Russell (the famous "cowboy artist" of Montana) by humorist Will Rogers, Amon G. Carter was convinced that the artist portrayed the true American West. In 1935 he borrowed money to buy nine Russell watercolors, and the founder and publisher of the *Fort Worth Star-Telegram* continued to collect western art until his death in 1955. Carter's will instructed that a museum be built to house his collection. And today the museum's collection of Frederic Remingtons and Charles Russells remains one of the most acclaimed anywhere. Philip Johnson designed the building, which opened in 1961, built of native Texas shellstone. Ten more intimate galleries open from the main gallery. The museum also houses a large reference library, a theater, and a bookstore.

The collection of American painting, sculpture, and photography is complemented by exhibitions and programs. The permanent collection also features works by Winslow Homer, Martin Johnson Heade, Seth Eastman, Jasper Cropsey, Albert Bierstadt, Thomas Moran, John Mix Stanley, and Frederick Church. Several examples of early 20th-century painting and sculpture are also found in the collection, among them works by Georgia O'Keeffe, John Martin, Stuart Davis, Ben Shahn, Charles Scheeler, Marsden Hartley, and Arthur Dove. Open Tuesday through Saturday, 10 A.M. to 5 P.M., and Sunday, 1 to 5:30 P.M. (closed Mondays); in summer to 8 P.M. on Tuesdays. Tours Tuesday through Saturday begin at 2 P.M. Group tours must be scheduled with the tour coordinator at least two weeks in advance. Free. Call (817) 738-6811.

Sid Richardson Collection of Western Art. 309 Main St., Sundance Sq.; (817) 332-6554. This one-room museum features 54 Remington and Russells and a small bookstore. Tues.-Fri. 10 A.M. to 5 P.M.; Sat. 11 A.M. to 6 P.M.; Sunday 1 to 5 P.M. Free.

Fort Worth Art Museum. 1309 Montgomery. Founded in 1901 as an art gallery in one room of the old public library by a group of patrons, it has evolved into a distinguished collection of 20th-century art. The collection has grown from its first acquisition of George Inness's *Approaching Storm* in 1904 to a collection including more than 3,000 works. Acquisitions in the late 1950s focused on modern masters, including Lyonel Feininger, Henri Matisse, Leonard Baskin, and Hans Hoffman.

The museum began to gain national and international recognition in the late 1960s and early '70s with the purchase of Picasso's *Suite Vollard* and *Femme Couchee Lisant* and the presentation of a Picasso exhibition jointly organized with the Dallas Museum of Fine Arts (now the Dallas

Museum of Art). The museum's collection includes significant works by Frank Stella, Clyfford Still, Donald Judd, Joseph Cornell, Mark Rothko, and Morris Louis. Specially commissioned pieces include major works by Robert Irwin, Robert Rauschenberg, and Red Grooms. In addition to exhibitions, other activities include lectures, slide programs, symposia, film series, adults' and children's programs, video and film productions in the public schools, scholarly publications, and arts programs. Open Tuesday to Saturday, 10 A.M. to 5 P.M. Call (817) 738-9215.

Fort Worth Museum of Science and History. 1501 Montgomery. Begun in 1941 at the Children's Museum, the Fort Worth Museum of Science and History has grown from two rooms in an elementary school to the largest museum of its kind in the Southwest. Its 88,000-sq.-ft. facility contains seven exhibit galleries, the largest museum school in the country, and the **Noble Planetarium,** where "Texas Skies" is run Tuesday–Friday at 1. The museum's collection of more than 100,000 specimens and artifacts ranges from fossils to computers. The collection also provides materials for the Museum School. During museum hours, area schoolchildren (more than 50,000 each year) attend curriculum-coordinated programs in science, history, and astronomy featuring hands-on contact with the teaching collection. In addition to the planetarium show and special light and sound production *Laser Magic,* the museum has a 30,000-sq.-ft. *Omni-Max Theater.* The special film projector creates images that visually surround the audience and carry it to the depths of the ocean and the far corners of the universe. The museum is open Monday through Thursday, 9 A.M. to 5 P.M., Friday and Saturday 9 A.M. to 8:30 P.M., and Sunday noon to 5 P.M. The museum is free. Noble Planetarium shows usually charge $2.50, $2 for "Texas Skies." Infants may not be admitted. The Laser Magic show is given Friday at 8:15, 9:30, and 10:45 P.M., and midnight, and Saturday at 7, 8:15, 9:30, 10:45, and midnight. The Omni-Max has 35 showings weekly; $4.75 for adults, $3.00 for children under 12 and seniors 55 and over. Call (817) 732-1631 for information on all museum facilities.

Kimbell Art Museum. 3333 Camp Bowie. Only into its second decade, the Kimbell is already famous for its collection of the world's art, ranging from the prehistoric to early 20th century, and the innovative building that houses it. The collection sweeps across most areas of European art, from prehistoric sculpture to Picasso, with a strong representation of old masters. The museum also has excellent examples of Oriental sculpture, screens, scrolls, and ceramics; pre-Colombian objects, and Africal sculpture. Artists represented include Cussio, El Greco, Rembrandt, Rubens, Goya, Gainsborough, Velazquez, Monet, Cezanne, and Matisse.

Often called the architect's masterpiece, the building was the last design personally completed by the late Louis I. Kahn. It has received top awards for design and construction, lighting, and engineering, as well as for its barrier-free facilities. Through the years the Kimbell has mounted numerous important touring exhibitions, ranging from the heralded *Impressionist and Post-Impressionist Paintings from the U.S.S.R.* to the record-setting showing of *The Great Bronze Age of China* to *The Votive Tradition: Treasures of Buddhist Sculpture from Japan.* Also *Chinese Ceramics: 1620–1683.* The museum is active in lecture programs, film series, children's classes, concerts, and special tours.

The Kimbell is administered by a private foundation established by the late Fort Worth industrialist Kay Kimbell. Upon his death in 1964, he left his entire fortune to the foundation to build the museum to house and expand his collection. His widow joined his will, leaving her share of the community property to the same ends. Facilities include a 180-seat auditorium, a regional conservation center, a bookstore, a superb art library (by reservation only), and a buffet service open for luncheons. Open Tuesday through Saturday, 10 A.M. to 5 P.M., and Sunday, 11 A.M. to 5 P.M. Call (817) 332–8451.

Cattlemen's Museum. 1301 W. 7th. Provides history and artifacts on the growth of the cattle industry from the 1800s to the present. Visitors learn the story of the industry from the evolution of the first American beef animal—the Texas longhorn—to the trail drives north to provide beef for the rest of the nation. Exhibits tell the story of the role of the woman in the beef industry as well as of the battles the cattle raisers have fought with fever ticks, natural disasters, and, most importantly, the rustler. It also tells the story of the origination of the brand inspector and the organization of the group that first employed him—the Texas and Southwestern Cattle Raisers Association. Included are all the tools of the cowboy's trade, from revolver to spurs, from branding iron to barbed wire. The museum presents short videotapes of the history of the older Texas ranches, including the Burnett Estates and the Waggoner Ranch. Interactive exhibits allow the visitor a hands-on experience of ranching in the past and present. Adjoining the museum is the Cattle Raisers Memorial Hall. Open Monday through Friday, 8:30 A.M. to 4:30 P.M. Free. Call 332–7064.

Exhibits and displays at the **Pate Museum of Transportation,** on U.S. 377 14 mi. southwest of Fort Worth near Cresson, feature antique, classic, and other special cars, military aircraft and artifacts, a railroad car and artifacts, and a Navy mine sweeper boat, to name some. Open Tuesday through Sunday, 9 A.M. to 5 P.M. Free. Call (817) 923–1924, ext. 275 ext. 323.

Tandy Archaeological Museum, A. Webb Roberts Library, Southwestern Baptist Theological Seminary. Study of early Biblical periods. Permanent collection of artifacts uncovered at Tel Batash-Timnah, Israel. Tours available on request. Free. (817) 923 1921. Monday to Friday, 8 A.M. to 5 P.M.

MUSIC. Dallas voters said yes in 1982 to a bond issue that will in September 1989 give citizens a new concert hall to join the Museum of Art as the second resident of the newly born Arts District a neighborhood on the northern edge of downtown, southeast of the Woodall Rodgers Fwy. between St. Paul and Routh (pronounced "Ruth") Sts. The future home of the **Dallas Symphony Orchestra** as well as a center for other musical and educational events, the new concert hall is called Morton H. Meyerson Symphony Center and received substantial gifts from private contributors. Architect I. M. Pei was commissioned to design the $80-million concert hall, and Russell Johnson is responsible for acoustical engineering. Presently, the DSO shares the Fair Park Music Hall with numerous events, including the Civic Opera (see below), meaning its season, beginning in September, is suspended until January in order to free the Music Hall for the October State Fair and the November opera season. Thursdays in June and July, the symphony's Discovery Series offers light classical concerts performed in the Majestic Theater, 1925 Elm Street. The symphony played to its first audience in 1900. Today it is made up of 99 musicians who perform every week of the year under the leadership of Eduardo Mata. The full season includes several musical series featuring classical and pops performances, appearances with the Dallas Opera, park concerts, youth concerts, and performances for the handicapped. Call 692–0203 for ticket information.

The **Dallas Civic Music Association** (871–1182) presents five to six programs each season, between September and May, in Majestic Theater. Since its founding in 1930 it has presented an annual series of outstanding musical artists to the community. The **Dallas Chamber Music Society** hosts concerts featuring music ensembles with performances in Caruth Auditorium. Call SMU (692–2000) and ask for the school of music. The Dallas Classic Guitar Society offers a fall season.

The **Dallas Jazz Society** at the Majestic (739–5975) sponsors an annual salute to Duke Ellington in April, as well as other special concerts.

The **Fort Worth Symphony Orchestra** performs in concert from late September through May at the Tarrant County Convention Center Theatre. The Chamber Orchestra performs at Ed Landreth auditorium on the Texas University (TCU) campus during the same time periods. For information call 921–2676. Fort Worth is also the home of the internationally touring, Grammy-winning **Texas Boys Choir**.

The **Johnnie High Country Music Revue,** is a fast-paced, quality country-music variety show presented every Saturday at 7 P.M. at Fort Worth's Will Rogers Auditorium, 3301 W. Lancaster. A part of country music since childhood, Johnnie High has auditioned more than 5,000 acts in the last eight years for his weekly show. Call 481–4518 or 332–0909 for information.

Arenas drawing the big-name concerts in Dallas are Reunion Arena, SMU's McFarlin Auditorium, and the Dallas Convention Center, and, in Fort Worth, the Tarrant County Convention Center. Some are staged outdoors at the Cotton Bowl.

Opera

The **Fort Worth Opera,** Texas' longest continuing opera company, will enter its 50th season in 1989. In addition to productions staged during the season at Tarrant County Convention Center Theatre, the opera has formed an educational adjunct, the **Southwestern Opera Theater,** which plays annually to 30,000 schoolchildren in the Metroplex. For ticket information on the season, which begins in November, call 737–0775.

Having celebrated its 30th anniversary in 1987, the **Dallas Opera** offers four productions from late October or early November through late December at the Music Hall in State Fair Park. For years the only place in America where Maria Callas would perform, the Dallas Opera afforded Franco Zefferelli, Joan Sutherland, and Montserrat Caballe their American debuts. Call for Majestic Theatre performance information. Box office, 871–0090.

DANCE. The **International Theatrical Arts Society** (TITUS), 3709 Blackburn, 528–5576, a presenting organization in its seventh season brings exciting movement and dance to the Dallas area with 10 performances annually.

DALLAS AND FORT WORTH

The first professional black dance company in Dallas, the **Dallas Black Dance Theatre,** employs a repertoire of jazz, contemporary, and classical ballet. Situated on the campus of Bishop College in conjunction with the South Dallas Academy, the company trains dancers from preschool ages through adult. Call 371-1170 for information on performances. Also keeping Dallas on its toes are the *Dancers Unlimited,* and the *Krassovska Ballet Jeunesse of Dallas* on the SMU campus.

The **Fort Worth Ballet** opens its season in October as well, at Tarrant County Convention Center Theatre. Call 921-6998 for performance information.

STAGE. DALLAS. Dallas is the center of most of the theatrical activity in the Metroplex. The $1 million **Dallas Theater Center,** at 3636 Turtle Creek Blvd., contains the only public theater designed by Frank Lloyd Wright. The grand Kalita Humphreys Theater and intimate Down Center Stage, with performances ranging from Shakespeare to modern, opened in 1959. A breeding ground for world-renowned talent, the Dallas Theater Center has brought along such playwrights as the late Preston Jones, whose *A Texas Trilogy* premiered in Dallas, went on to set box-office records at the Kennedy Center in Washington, D.C., and won a Golden Apple Award on Broadway. Call 526-8857 for information.

Theatre Three, at 2800 Routh in the Quadrangle, was founded in 1961 by Norma Young and Jac Alder. Featuring the new as well as classics, today's performances range from children's plays to musicals, comedies, and dramas. This theater in the round seats approximately 250. Several TV and film stars got their starts here, including Morgan Fairchild and Ronnie Claire Edwards. Call 871-3300 for information.

Dallas Repertory Theatre, now in its 20th season in its own building at NorthPark, turns in five productions each year. Casting is done through open auditions, with Equity members performing leading roles. Call 369-8966 for information.

The **Dallas Summer Musicals** are staged at State Fair Music Hall, 1st Ave. and Parry in State Fair Park. Broadway and Hollywood stars perform in 8 to 10 shows. Since its first season in 1941, the musicals have presented such historic moments as Gene Kelly's return to the stage after 33 years and the musical-comedy debuts of Donald O'Connor, Patti Page, and Rock Hudson. Productions range from one-man shows, such as Rich Little, to full musical productions, such as *Big River.* Call 691-7200 for information. With as many as 17 performances, a **Shakespeare festival** also is produced on the grounds of Fair Park in June, though plans are in the making for a permanent performance home.

Southern Methodist University in Dallas is home to the **Margo Jones Theatre** and the **Bob Hope Theatre.** The U.S.A. Film Festival, an annual series highlighting U.S. films and filmmakers and honoring guest directors with film retrospectives, is presented in the Inwood Theatre. For more information call 692-2573.

In addition to performances by the resident acting company focusing on contemporary American theater, **Stage No. 1, Greenville Avenue Theatre,** 2914 Greenville, in Dallas, hosts other performing arts. Call 760-9542.

Built in 1921 as the headquarters of the Interstate Theatre chain, the baroque movie palace called the **Majestic Theatre,** 1925 Elm, featured famous vaudeville acts and movies of the days. After the theater was donated to the city of Dallas, funds were raised through a bond issue and private subscription to restore the building. Local dance, opera, theater, and concert agencies, as well as touring productions, use the multipurpose performing-arts hall.

FORT WORTH. Caravan of Dreams, opened in 1983, is a performing arts center including a spacious nightclub on the ground floor, a second-story theater/dance studio, and a spectacular open-air rooftop bar featuring a dome filled with many rare cacti. There is live music five nights weekly and bookings of world-class jazz musicians. Includes a 24-track MCI studio and film studio. London's *Wire* magazine named Caravan of Dreams "The Place to be in 1988." 312 Houston St., downtown; (817) 877-3000. **Casa Manana** puts on Broadway musicals, concerts, and plays in the country's first permanent musical arena theater (1958). At 3101 W. Lancaster in Amon Carter Square near Fort Worth's famous museums, this theater in the round offers a full summer season of road shows, featuring top names as well as local professionals. It is said a critic and former skeptic once said of Billy Rose's original, lavish outdoor playhouse: "Only two things live up to the claims of their press agents—the Grand Canyon and Fort Worth's Casa Manana. "Call 332-6221 for information.

The highly acclaimed **Hip Pocket Theatre** takes its productions outdoors at Oak Acres Amphitheatre June 10 till November. Spring performances are staged upstairs at the White Elephant, 108 E. Exchange Ave. in the stockyards district. 1620 Las Vegas Trail N. Customers are doubly satisfied: barbecue is served before each performance. Call 927-2833 for information and reservations.

Home of the **Fort Worth Theatre,** the $1.25 million **William Edrington Scott Theatre,** at 3505 W. Lancaster, is open for guided tours by appointment. Call 738-6509. Plays and film series are given year-round.

Fort Worth's summer **Shakespeare** series is given in Trinity Park.

SHOPPING. DALLAS. There's no denying out-of-towners' fascination with *Neiman-Marcus,* especially at the original location, downtown at 1618 Main (at Ervay). The fourth-floor antiques are a special draw. Expect to compete storewide with hordes of locals during Last Call bargain days in late January and July.

The consensus on the town's best buy on Western boots is at down-to-earth *Mistletoe Boot Shop,* 942 E. Jefferson in Oak Cliff (I-35 south to the Jefferson exit, then one block).

The fashion-conscious woman can be seen maneuvering in the constantly changing "designer row" shops along Lovers La. between Inwood and Preston Roads in North Dallas. But the latest entries in the shopping sweepstakes are in the Galleria, Dallas Parkway north of LBJ Freeway in Far North Dallas, with such names as *Saks, Marshall Field, Gump's,* and *Tiffany's.*

If Galleria's ice rink is too crowded, try the one at Prestonwood Town Center, or at the Plaza of the America's Hotel. to the north at Dallas Parkway and Belt Line, with *Neiman-Marcus, Dillard's* and *Lord & Taylor.* Between Galleria and Prestonwood are *Sakowitz Village* and a bevy of eating establishments. Valley View Mall, to the east of Galleria on LBJ Freeway between Montfort and Preston, offers *Foley's, Dillard's, Bloomingdale's,* and *Macy's.*

Probably the most central shopping mall in Dallas, decorative NorthPark Center, at Northwest Highway (Loop 12) and North Central Expressway (U.S. 75), is home to *Neiman-Marcus, Dillard's,* and *Lord & Taylor,* in addition to the Dallas Repertory Theatre. Kitty-corner to the mall at Central and Park Lane is Caruth Plaza, featuring sporty *Abercrombie & Fitch.*

A few blocks south of NorthPark and east of Central Expressway is Old Town mall at Lovers La. and Greenville Avenue in the heart of the North Dallas singles' stamping grounds. Old Town's specialty stores are bounded by a TGI Friday's and an all-night Tom Thumb supermarket.

The first shopping center of its kind in the country, Highland Park Shopping Center, Preston at Mockingbird in Highland Park, offers probably the swankiest *Foley's* and *Pierre Deaux* department stores in town. But parking at this Spanish-style center can be a problem, especially when the movie crowd moves in. Look for antiques at the *McKinney Avenue Market* at 2710 McKinney Ave.

Arts and crafts aficionados can get their fix at, to name three centers, the *Craft Compound,* 6617 Snider Plaza near Lovers La. in Highland Park, with its crafts shops, galleries, antiques, and folk art; *Olla Podrida,* at 12215 Coit, west of Central Expressway between Forest La. and LBJ Freeway, an old barn converted into an artsy two-story "melting pot" of specialty shops; and the *Quadrangle,* 2800 Routh between Cedar Springs and McKinney near downtown in a historic section of Oak Lawn, with its Indian pueblo-style grouping of shops known for their pottery, jewelry, glassworks, baskets, and candles.

Traders Village, 2602 Mayfield Rd. in Grand Prairie, is a 106-acre Texas-size flea market where everything imaginable is bought and sold from 100 booths every Saturday and Sunday from 8:00 A.M. to dusk. Call (214) 647-2331 for information.

Other major shopping centers in Dallas include: Big Town Mall, U.S. 80 and 67 east in Mesquite; Town East Mall, LBJ Freeway at Town East Blvd. in Mesquite; Casa Linda Plaza, Garland Rd. and Buckner east of White Rock Lake in East Dallas; Red Bird Mall, east of Duncanville at 3662 W. Camp Wisdom and U.S. 67 South; Richardson Square Mall, 501 S. Plano Rd. in Richardson; and Irving Mall, west in Irving at Texas 183 and Belt Line.

Earmarked for a $2-million expansion to be completed 1989-90, *Dallas Farmer's Market,* in the southeast corner of downtown, offers visitors a taste of the Texas truck-farming tradition. Depending on the season, trucks brim with tomatoes, corn, watermelons, potatoes, and grapefruit, among the countless offerings on 8.5 acres of huge sheds. Get there *early;* 1010 So. Pearl Expressway; 6-6 7 days a week. Call (214) 748-2082 for information.

Some 500,000 professional buyers from across the country and around the world converge on the Texas-size *Dallas Market Center* each year to spend $5 billion (wholesale) for residential and contract furnishings, gifts, decorative accessories, leisure goods, jewelry, toys, and apparel. At 2100 Stemmons Freeway, Market Center (655-6100) encompasses the Apparel Mart, the Decorative Center, the Home Furnishings Center, Market Hall, the Trade Mart, and the World Trade Center. Plantings and contemporary sculpture have been placed in and around the various buildings. Only the ground floor is open to the public.

Both Dallas and Fort Worth have plenty of exciting art galleries covering a range of specialties. Check the weekend-guide sections in the Friday editions of the *Dallas Morning News* and the *Dallas Times Herald* and the latest issue of *D* magazine for current offerings. Area universities and colleges have their own galleries too.

FORT WORTH. Fort Worth, where the West begins, can stagger the Western-wear shopper with sheer numbers. For example, the *Justin Boot Company Outlet,* three blocks south of downtown at 717 W. Vickery Blvd., houses thousands of wholesale overstock boots from its Fort Worth factory; *Luskey's,* downtown at 101 Houston, is a sure-find in western threads and several brands of boots, and *Shepler's,* south of I-30 in Arlington at 2500 E. Centennial Dr., offers more than an acre of floor space. The Fort Worth Stockyards area, Main and Exchange on the North Side, is home to specialty shops offering western apparel and merchandise of the historic cattle era.

A slice of downtown Fort Worth's present facelift, Sundance Square, with its turn-of-the-century architecture, features new restaurants, shops, and night-spots in low-rise buildings.

Cowtown does not lack for malls, either. At Hulen Mall, in southwest Fort Worth at 4800 S. Hulen St., *Foley's* and good snacks are the bywords. *Neiman-Marcus* is the calling card for Ridgmar Mall, 2060 Green Oaks at I-30 in west Fort Worth. Not to be confused with Ridgmar, the Ridglea shopping area, featuring the *Stripling and Cox* department store, lies to the southeast on Camp Bowie (U.S. 377/U.S. 80 Business) between I-30 and the Weatherford traffic circle.

Other major shopping centers in the Fort Worth area include:

Tandy Center, downtown at Throckmorton and Weatherford; Downtown Cowtown, 813 E. 9th St. (weekends only); Fort Worth Town Center, I-35 at Seminary Dr.; Market Center, 4950 Highway 377 South (weekends only); North Hills Mall, 7624 Grapevine Hwy.; and Northeast Mall, northeast in Hurst at Texas 183/121 at I-820. In Arlington: Forum 303, 2900 Pioneer Parkway; Six Flags Mall, 411 Six Flags Dr.; and Carriage Plaza, 900 Copeland Road at Texas 157.

DINING OUT IN DALLAS. Partly because of antiquated liquor laws, which held sway until 1972, one must pay "membership fees" to drink in many establishments outside the "wet" areas of town.) Dallas restaurants have increased in number and quality there are 5700 restaurants in the Dallas Area. the first, astronomically; the second, in a more measured fashion. Many of these new establishments are cynical products of marketing, and they tend to disappear as quickly as they materialize.

Finding a good restaurant in Dallas can be exponentially more difficult than that old needle-haystack search we've heard about all our lives. At least needles *look* bright and shiny, and haystraws don't have big-budget advertising campaigns designed to make them appear to be something they are not. Unfortunately, honesty is not the house policy in many local restaurants. If it were against the law to impersonate a restaurateur, most Dallas food handlers would be in jail. The odds are against you when you walk into any of the 4,000-odd restaurants in the Dallas area expecting to sit down to a rewarding dining experience. But a few restaurants are the product of commitment to good eating.

The search for a good restaurant is made even more difficult because most restaurateurs are attuned to Dallas diners' tendency to equate price—and sometimes pomposity—with culinary excellence. It is one of the central components of the Dallas psyche that you get what you pay for; therefore, a meal that costs more than your wristwatch *has* to be good. This notion has spawned a legion of restaurants that might best called pseudo-Continental, usually run by counterfeit Gallics whose cooking skills have yet to equal their self-esteem.

Of Dallas's high-ticket choices, Routh Street Cafe, Enjolie, and The Mansion provide the most reliably extraordinary dining experience. Restaurants of this type have ever-escalating tabs that are correspondingly extraordinary. Dallas's big-deal restaurant tabs rival New York's, which is to be considered if one isn't on an expense account, as many of the patrons are. Be wary, especially, of off-the-menu options.

To eat with a view, consider the Hilton's Harper's Restaurant and Club; stick with drinks at the Hyatt Regency's Antares, Reunion Tower.

As for native fare, don't expect trail-wagon specialties on every corner in Dallas. Certainly, Texana is available, at local favorites like Hoffbrau Steaks. But Dallas's true indigenous cuisine subdivides into barbecue, southern, and Tex-Mex (which is particularly cheap, satisfying, and addictive).

Dallasites tend to take these areas for granted; they pride themselves on two other counts: the nouvelle and haute cuisine of the city's most pricey restaurants and the range of sometimes obscure ethnic food in the most inexpensive holes in the wall.

Good restaurants are spread throughout the city (with the partial exception of Oak Cliff, which suffers from a no-alcohol, low-income history). North Dallas, the area between the LBJ Freeway and Belt Line Rd. near the Dallas Parkway in the township of Addison, is the site of the biggest boom. There are a few jewels in the midst of the paste flash and glitter, but too many North Dallas restaurants ride on their plush ambience.

Other restaurant-dense areas are Greenville Ave., which spans the city from north to south parallel to North Central Expy.; Lower Greenville (below Mockingbird) tends to funk; Upper Greenville (considered to be part of North Dallas) caters to more upscale, though not necessarily more discerning, tastes. McKinney Ave., near downtown, offers a small group of diverse options. And downtown Dallas has seen a restaurant boom of sorts with the active revitalization of the West End Historical District. In addition, one block east of the intersection of I–35 and Walnut Hill Lane, you can find a cluster of diverse restaurants. For a taste of ethnic Dallas, the intersection of Maple and Wycliff is the center of Mexican restaurants and shops. Tex-Mex is ubiquitous, with its combination plates of tacos, enchiladas, tamales, and chalupas.

Both the *Dallas Times Herald* and *The Dallas Morning News* publish restaurant listings each Friday; the *Morning News's* are more extensive. *D Magazine* also publishes monthly lists and rates a wide variety of restaurants.

The price classifications of the following restaurants, from inexpensive to deluxe, are based on the cost of an average three-course dinner for one person for food alone; beverages, tax, and tip would be extra. *Inexpensive,* less than $8; *Moderate,* $8 to $15; *Expensive,* $15 to $30; and *Deluxe,* more than $30.

Abbreviations for credit cards are: AE, American Express; CB, Carte Blanche; DC, Diners Club; MC, MasterCard; V, Visa. Most restaurants that do not accept credit cards will cash traveler's checks; few, however, will honor personal checks. Abbreviations for meal codes are: B, breakfast; L, lunch; D, dinner. Since restaurant hours and days of closing often change, you should call first to confirm.

All telephone numbers are area code 214.

American-International

Deluxe

Beau Nash. Hotel Crescent Court, 400 Crescent Court; 871–3200. The menu features innovative American provincial cuisine; rack of lamb is a winner. The casually elegant setting with one room overlooking open kitchens and the other overlooking the courtyard, makes it popular with natives and visitors alike. B, L, D, Monday through Sunday. AE, DC, MC, V.

Enjolie. Dallas Marriott Mandalay at Las Colinas, 221 S. Las Colinas Blvd., Irving; 556–0800. The Mandalay's top-of-the-line restaurant offers discreetly classy surroundings. Don't miss the knockout pheasant mousse and the decadent desserts. The complimentary cheese tray and selection of petit fours add to the experience without adding to the tab. L, D, Monday through Saturday. AE, MC, V. (Also under *French.*)

The Mansion. 2821 Turtle Creek Blvd., North Dallas; 526–2121. The Mansion's elegant setting and late-night supper make it a favorite stopping point for visiting celebrities. The Dean Fearing-consulted menu is perhaps the best nouvelle American cuisine (with a southwestern flavor) in town. Tie and jacket required for men. B, L, D, daily. High tea is served Monday through Friday in the Promenade. AE, DC, MC, V.

Routh Street Cafe. 3005 Routh St. (at Cedar Springs); 871–7161. A creative, changing menu served in an austere, lovely setting adds up to Dallas' most exciting dining experience. Tuesday through Saturday. AE, DC, MC, V. Reservations required.

Expensive

Ewald's. At the Stoneleigh, 2927 Maple Ave., 75201; 871–2523. This chef-owned restaurant is a longtime favorite of Dallas natives, who come for the high-quality veal and beef dishes. Five-course fixed price menu. The decor is elegant. D, B, L, daily. AE, DC, MC, V.

Old Warsaw. 2610 Maple Ave., north of downtown; 528–0032. In its heyday, the peak dining experience in Dallas. Still worth it for the extraordinary, classy-bordello plushness of the setting. Stick to simple choices of French cuisine though; the elaborate offerings are disappointing. D, daily. AE, DC, MC, V.

Moderate

Baby Routh. 2708 Routh; 871–2345. Offspring of Routh Street Cafe. One of the best deals in terms of quality-to-price ratio. Regional southwestern cuisine. Charming setting. L, D, daily. AE, DC, MC, V.

The Bistroquet. Adolphus Hotel, 1321 Commerce; 742–8200. This English club look-alike is across the lobby from the far more famous French Room. The food rarely comes close to the French Room's heights, but neither do the prices. It's still terrific for hotel food. Breakfast, though, is distinctly overpriced. B, Monday through Saturday; brunch, Sunday; L, D, Monday through Saturday. AE, DC, MC, V.

Café d'Or. Dallas Marriott Mandalay at Las Colinas, 221 S. Las Colinas Blvd., Irving (west of Dallas, off Rte. 114); 556–0800. Appetizers and salads are the standouts at this ambitious, reasonably priced, casual restaurant of the Mandalay. B, daily; L, Monday through Saturday; D, daily. AE, DC, MC, V.

Jennivine. 3605 McKinney Ave., north of downtown; 528–6010. The service and food are uneven, but the imaginative, seafood-oriented English and French menu, which changes daily, keeps patrons coming back to this relaxed spot. Good selection of wines by the glass. Small patio for outdoor dining. L, D, Monday through Saturday. AE, DC, MC, V.

Inexpensive

Bennigan's. 2410 Walnut Hill (at I-35); 350–3127. 5260 Belt Line (across from Prestonwood Mall); 233–2107. 8139 Park Lane; 696–2080. 721 N. Watson, Arlington; 640–6088. This bar/restaurant chain features munchy fare and an intensive singles scene. L, D, daily. AE, DC, MC, V.

Bronx. 3835 Cedar Springs Rd., north of Oak Lawn Ave. 521–5821. Not a bargain but a blessing for late-night sustenance, especially as a source of good coffee and dessert. Daily specials are good bets. Sophisticated, comfortable neighborhood bar. Substantially gay patronage. L, D, Monday through Friday; D, Saturday, Sunday brunch. AE, DC, MC, V.

Dalt's. 5100 Belt Line, east of Dallas North Parkway in Addison. Suite 410; 386–9078. A marble-and-brass re-creation of drugstore soda-fountain decor. The food is munchie material, not the stuff of serious dining. L, D, daily. AE, DC, MC, V.

Austrian

Expensive

Belvedere. 4242 Lomo Alto Dr. at Crestpark, north of downtown; 528–6510. A sibling of the Chimney (see below) that almost, but not quite, lives up to the Chimney's standards and specializes in Swiss and Austrian cuisine. The atmosphere is less intimate than the Chimney's but still warm, with chandeliers, a fireplace, and live music. At both restaurants, appetizers and desserts are eminently skippable. L, D, Monday through Saturday. AE, DC, MC, V.

The Chimney. Willow Creek Shopping Center, 9739 N. Central Expressway at Walnut Hill exit, North Dallas; 369–6466. The Rehsteak Chimney—astonishingly tender, subtly sauced venison tournedos, served at dinner only—is a local legend. The candlelight-and-soft-piano-music setting is quietly classy. L, D, Monday through Saturday. AE, DC, MC, V.

Barbecue and Chili

Inexpensive

Big Al's. 3212 Inwood (near Cedar Springs); 350–2649. Traditional barbecue with all the trimmings (slaw, potato salad, beans, and so forth). L, D, Monday through Saturday. AE, and personal checks.

Blue Ribbon. 316 Hillside Village (Mockingbird at Abrams); 823–5524. Blue Ribbon features brisket, ham, sausage, and ribs in a cafeteria-style setting. The sauce is tangy and the music is country. L, D, Monday through Saturday. No credit cards but personal checks accepted.

Gene's. 3002 Canton; 386–6568. This downtown spot calls itself "home of the healthy plate." They're referring to the size of the typical serving, not the surgeon general's opinion. The offerings are, however, commendably grease free. The sausage in particular is terrific. No liquor. L, Monday through Friday. No credit cards.

Salih's. 4801 Belt Line, Addison (north); 387–2900. One of the most cleancut, pleasant barbecue experiences for the uninitiated. Faultless beef, sausage, ribs, chicken, and ham are served in a 1950s diner setting. Beer, wine. L, D, Monday through Saturday. MC, V.

Sonny Bryan's. 2202 Inwood Road, west of Dallas North Tollway near Harry Hines Blvd.; 357–7120. The sauce, which is legendary in Dallas, is the thing here. A cross section of Dallasites always crowds the tiny, dingy interior, where school-desk tops substitute for tables. Can seat only a few, but the rest gladly stand. Go early; the place closes up when the meat's all gone. Beer. L, daily. No credit cards. Personal checks accepted.

Cafeterias

Inexpensive

Highland Park Cafeteria. 4611 Cole Ave. in North Dallas; 526–3801. A local institution. HPC is probably the best place to sample reasonably priced southern-style home cooking. The array of dishes must be seen to be believed. Lines are always long, but they move quickly. (Also at 5100 Belt Line, 934–8025.) L, D, Monday through Saturday. AE, MC, V.

Luby's Cafeteria. Many locations; see the Yellow Pages. Above-average cafeteria food. L, D, daily. No credit cards.

Wyatt's Cafeterias. Many locations; see the Yellow Pages. Good cafeteria food. No credit cards.

Chinese

Although there are Chinese restaurants around every corner in Dallas, most are mediocre, relying on canned vegetables and MSG. Four stand out as exceptions: *Uncle Tai's, Forbidden City, Fang-ti China,* and *Bamboo Pavilion.*

Expensive

Uncle Tai's. Level 3, Galleria, Dallas Parkway at LBJ, far north Dallas; 934–9998. High-priced, high-quality fare in an austerely chic setting. Don't miss the sauteed sliced pheasant (or the crispy walnuts for dessert). L, D, Monday-Sunday. AE, DC, MC, V.

DALLAS AND FORT WORTH

Moderate

Bamboo Pavilion. 1790 Promenade Center, on Coit between Belt Line Road and Arapaho, in Richardson, north of Far North Dallas; 680–0599. This sibling of Szechwan Pavilion offers the same high-quality, moderately priced fare in a nicer setting. Must-try: walnut shrimp. L, D, daily. Alcohol served to members only. AE, DC, MC, V.

Forbidden City. 5290 Belt Line, in Addison, far north; 960–2999. Unusually classy decor is the backdrop for carefully prepared Szechwan and Mandarin dishes. L, D, daily. Full bar. AE, DC, MC, V.

Han-Chu. Caruth Plaza, 9100 N. Central Expressway (at Park La.); 691–0900. Sophisticated decor and classy service belie its moderate prices. Go for the shredded pork with ginger sauce. L, D, daily. Full bar. AE, DC, MC, V.

Szechwan Pavilion. 8411 Preston Rd. at Northwest Highway, North Dallas. 368–4303. Szechwan Pavilion has a crisp, inviting atmosphere and the food is far above average. Alcohol served to members only. L, D, daily. AE, MC, V.

Inexpensive

Fang-ti China. Twin Bridge Shopping Center, 6752 Shady Brook Ln. near Northwest Hwy., North Dallas; 987–3877. Open until six in the morning on weekends (and merely till 4:00 A.M. on weekdays), Fangti's above-average food starts to look great in the wee hours, considering the alternatives, which are nearly nonexistent in Dallas. Chances are good of meeting Fang-ti herself, who is proud of her status as the only female Chinese chef in the city. L, Monday–Friday, D daily. Serves late. Full bar. AE, DC, MC, V.

Texaco Lunch Box. 3801 Ross Ave. (at Washington Ave.), downtown; 821–5036. The food is ordinary fast-food caliber but worth a visit so you can say you've been there. Where else can you fill up with unleaded and eggrolls to go? (Texaco Lunch Box sells gasoline and lunches.) L, Monday through Friday. No credit cards.

Czechoslovakian

Moderate

Bohemia. 2810 N. Henderson, east of North Central Expy., North of downtown; 826–6209. Hearty, well-prepared eastern-European food is served in delicately charming surroundings. Don't miss the homemade apple strudel. Beer, wine; no cocktails. D, Tuesday through Sunday. AE, DC, MC, V.

Delicatessens

Whatever you say about Dallas, you can't say that it's a great city for deli food.

Inexpensive

Bagelstein's. 8104 Spring Valley (north, above LBJ Fwy. 635); 234–3787. Bagelstein's is notable for its seven kinds of bagels baked daily. No liquor. L, Tuesday through Sunday; D, Tuesday through Saturday. No credit cards.

Kuby's. 6601 Snider Plaza, Hillcrest Ave. at Lovers Ln.; 363–2231. This German-style sandwich and sausage purveyor is a Dallas institution. (Translation; it's nearly always crowded.) No liquor, L, Monday through Saturday. MC, V.

Ethiopian

Inexpensive

Queen of Sheba. 3527 McKinney (at Lemmon); 521–0491. The unknown terrain of Ethiopian food, which is unusual and *very* spicy, is not for the faint of heart. Expect to spend some time here; the philosophy behind the service is very unhurried. Beer, wine; no cocktails. L, D, daily. AE, DC, MC, V.

Red Sea. 3851 Cedar Spring, 520–9153. The food and service are much like Blue Nile's, but the coffeeshop-like setting is less appealing. Full bar. D, daily. MC, V.

Fast Food

In addition to the standard national franchises, two local institutions are noteworthy:

Schlotzky's is renowned for its multi-ingredient (including ham, lunch meat, cheese, black olives, lettuce, tomato, and onion) sandwich served on home-baked bread. 5601 W. Lovers La.; 351–6587. 3529 McKinney Ave.; 528–3480. (Beer at preceding two.) 1503 Commerce; 744–3176. 13531 Montfort; 233–7554. 3203 W. Camp Wisdom; 339–9784. 13551 N. Central Expressway; 234–4249. 1734 S. Buckner; 391–3443.

Gonzalez (see *Mexican*) serves creditable, drive-through Tex-Mex breakfasts, lunches, and dinners.

Great Outdoor Sub Shops. Scattered throughout Dallas; serve large variety of submarine sandwiches. L, D daily.

French

Deluxe

Café Royal. 650 N. Pearl (Plaza of the Americas); 979–9000. The warm, rich decor sets the stage for nouvelle cuisine at its best (when the kitchen is on). Veal steak with lime butter is always a sure bet, though. Discreet piano music adds to the feeling of leisurely luxury (sometimes too leisurely on the part of the service). L, Monday through Friday; D, Monday through Saturday. Prix fixe menu available. AE, DC, MC, V.

French Room. Adolphus Hotel, 1321 Commerce St.; 742–8200. The most luxurious restaurant in town; stunning baroque decor and good-to-great nouvelle cuisine. Langoustine bisque for an appetizer and the feuilletee of seasonal fruit for dessert are musts. D, Monday through Saturday. AE, DC, MC, V.

Expensive

Actuelle. The Quadrangle, 2800 Routh; 855–0440. Great people-watching spot; excellent service and imaginative cuisine with a touch of the Southwest. L, Monday through Friday; D, Monday through Saturday. AE, DC, MC, V.

DALLAS AND FORT WORTH

L'Ambiance. 2408 Cedar Springs Rd., north of downtown; 748–1291. This former filling station is now an accepted bastion of nouvelle cuisine. Salads and soups are standouts. L, Monday through Friday; D, Monday through Saturday 720–5249.. AE, DC, MC, V.

Pyramid Room. Fairmont Hotel, Akard at Rose Ave., downtown; AE, DC, MC, V. Dallas's first sophisticated Continental restaurant has spawned many successors but is still worth a visit. The atmosphere of opulence is highlighted by maximum pampering, L, Monday through Friday; D, daily.

The Riviera. 7709 Inwood; 351–0094. A see-and-be-seen spot. The setting is beautiful and the food dependably first-rate. Scrumptious salmon and sea scallops in a wine sauce and killer desserts are musts. The only drawback: extremely noisy. D, daily. AE, DC, MC, V.

Les Saisons. 165 Turtle Creek Village Shopping Center, Oak Lawn Ave. at Blackburn St., north of downtown; 528–1102. Traditional French food and atmosphere at their best. L, D, daily. Full bar. AE, DC, MC, V.

Hamburgers

Inexpensive

Chip's. 4501 N. Central Expressway; 526–1092. Basic burgers done right and served in nifty surroundings. Beer, wine; no cocktails. L, D, Monday through Saturday. AE, MC, V.

The Points are essentially bars, but they serve a huge, locally renowned burger. *The Point After,* 5724 E. Lovers; 691–3525. L, D, daily. *The Wycliff Point,* 2525 Wycliff; 528–2030. L, D, daily *Northwest Point,* 2051 W. Northwest Hwy.; 869–2477. L, D daily. *The High Point,* 1201 Greenville; 437–9196. L, D daily. AE, MC, V.

Snuffer's. 3526 Greenville, northeast Dallas; 826–6850. This pub-restaurant has a limited menu offering one of the best—and largest—burgers in town. An order of the homemade fries will easily do for two; the size is ridiculously huge. Full bar. Serves late. L, D, daily. AE, MC, V.

Health Food

Moderate

Francis Simun's. 1507 N. Garrett St; 824–4910. Very upscale for a health-food restaurant: pretty pastel decor and classical background music. Great house salad, superb whole-grain-crust quiche, creamy apricot mousse. Beer, wine. L, D, Monday through Saturday D, Sunday. AE.

Inexpensive

Wholefoods Market and Cafe. 2218 Greenville, Dallas; 828–0052. Austin-style (laid-back) health food establishment and juice bar with limited, flavorful fare. Try a fresh papaya smoothie and black-bean nachos. Beer, wine. L, D daily. MC, V.

Harthomp & Moran Natural Foods Grocery. 9191 Forest Ln., far north Dallas; 231–6083. Outstanding fare, especially fruit salad. Awkward seating. Same owners as H&M Natural Foods Grocery. No liquor. L, Monday through Sunday. AE, DC, MC, V.

Kalachandji's. 5430 Gurley Ave., east Dallas; 821-1048. It's Hare Krishna-run, but don't let that scare you away. For set price get your choice from the hot buffet of a delicious Indian dinner. Eat in the courtyard, surrounded by stained glass. No liquor. D, Tuesday through Saturday. D, Sunday buffet. AE, DC, MC, V.

Indian

Moderate

India Palace. 13360 Preston; 392-0190. Excellent Indian cuisine with food spiced to order. Try the tandoor-baked meats. Atmosphere is polished. L, D, daily. Full bar, membership required. AE, DC, MC, V.

Inexpensive

Kebab-n-Kurry. 401 N. Central Expressway (between Belt Line and Arapaho), Richardson, north of Dallas; 231-5556. This tiny, charming restaurant is one of the best finds in the area. Beautifully authentic Indian food is served in an unlikely strip shopping-center location. No liquor. L, D, daily. AE, MC, V.

Italian

Expensive

Mario's. 135 Turtle Creek Village Shopping Center, Oak Lawn Ave. at Blackburn St., north of downtown; 521-1135. If one of your party wants Italian and another wants Continental fare, Mario's is the compromise of choice. Far more formal—and expensive—than any other Italian restaurant in town. L, D, daily. AE, DC, MC, V.

311 Lombardi's. 311 Market; 747-0322. This West End restaurant does well on both the personality and food fronts. Congenial waiters and first-class Italian fare make reservations a must. Veal and pasta best bets. L, Monday through Saturday; D, daily. AE, DC, MC, V.

La Tosca. 7713 Inwood Rd., south of Lovers Ln., North Dallas; 352-8373. The black-and-white decor is almost new wave in its minimalist chic. Homemade pasta and offbeat specialties such as octopus salad are featured. D, Tuesday through Sunday. AE, DC, MC, V.

Moderate

Bugatti. 2574 Walnut Hill Ln., northwest Dallas; 350-2470. A terrific value: Outstanding pasta and good veal dishes are served in pretty and relaxing surroundings at reasonable prices. Tortellini alla crema, fettucine della casa, and the mushroom soup are must-order items. Skip the forgettable desserts, though. L, Monday through Friday; D, Monday through Saturday. AE, DC, MC, V.

Cremona Bistro. 3136 Routh St. in Chelsea Square Shopping Center, north of downtown; 871-1115. Fine, no-frills Italian fare in pleasantly spare surroundings: ladder-back chairs, white tablecloths, and hardwood floors—and that's about it. The pasta consistently outshines the veal. L, D, Monday through Saturday. AE, DC, MC, V.

Nero's Italian. 2104 Greenville; 826-6376. Nero's is small, chic and made for tête-à-têtes. Pizza to veal chops and an extensive wine list are

DALLAS AND FORT WORTH

also major draws. Other gourmet Italian dishes available. D, Monday through Sunday. AE, MC, V.

Inexpensive

Acapella. 2508 Maple Ave.; 871–2262. This restaurant is situated in a remodeled Victorian home, where the pizza is in the tradition of L.A.'s Spago—with unusual toppings. L, D, daily. AE, MC, V.

Ciao. Cedar Springs at Throckmorton; 521–0110. An open kitchen and an engaging, art-deco decor add to the appeal of the pizza-intensive menu here. L, D, daily. AE, MC, V, and personal checks.

Japanese

Expensive

Kobe Steaks. Quorum Plaza Shopping Center, Belt Line Rd. at Dallas Parkway, north Dallas; 934–8150. Plush, contemporary Japanese-style steakhouse; chef prepares meals at hibachi tables. D, daily. AE, DC, MC, V.

Moderate

Mr. Sushi, 4860 Belt Line Rd. (at Inwood Rd.), Addison; 385–0168. Sushi and cooked Japanese dishes are featured at this lively, upscale restaurant. L, Monday through Friday. D, daily. AE, DC, MC, V.

Sakura. 7402 Greenville Ave. (in Old Vickery Park), North Dallas; 361–9282. Newly reopened and remodeled, with tatami and American-style seating. Aficionados say the sushi bar is the best in town. D, daily. AE, DC, MC, V.

Inexpensive

Fuji-Ya. 13050 Coit (at LBJ Fwy. 635, North Dallas); 690–8396. Go for the authentic food; the setting is very casual. Liquor with membership. L, D, daily except Monday. AE, MC, V.

Mexican

Moderate

Casa Rosa. 165 Inwood Village Shopping Center, Lovers Ln. at Inwood Road; 350–5227. Out-of-the-ordinary Tex-Mex in an attractive setting, much like Café Cancún. L, Monday through Friday; D, daily. Major credit cards.

Chiquita. 4514 Travis St., Highland Park; 520–7623. Ordinary tacos and bontanos and more interesting, more expensive Mexico City-style specialties such as a rich, cheesy tortilla soup and filete a la Chiquita (filet mignon Mexican-style). Bright, pastel decor. L, D, Monday through Saturday. AE, MC, V.

La Calle Doce. 415 W. 12th Street; 941–4304. A rare find in the Oak Cliff section. In a pretty restored home. The Mexican specialties are better than the Tex-Mex combination plates. Liquor with membership. L, Monday through Friday; D, Monday through Saturday. AE, DC, MC, V.

Loma Luna. 4131 Lomo Alto Dr., Park Cities; 559–4011. Pretty, Santa Fe style setting. Imaginative dishes far removed from city's standard Tex-Mex: enchiladas verdes (chicken enchiladas with green tomatillo sauce), corn-cheese, blue corn tortillas, soup, black beans. L, D, daily. AE, DC, MC, V.

Mario & Alberto's. 425 Preston Valley Center (LBJ Freeway 635 at Preston, North Dallas); 980–7296. Same owners and menu as Chiquita. As at its sibling restaurant, the smart money is on the Mexico City-style dishes rather than the very ordinary Tex-Mex. Liquor with membership. L, D, Monday through Saturday. AE, DC, MC, V.

Montezuma's. 3232 McKinney Ave., north of downtown; 559–3010. The consistently acceptable menu (offering standard Tex-Mex as well as more off-the-beaten-path choices), pretty setting (including an outdoor patio), and close-to-downtown location attract a steady crowd. L, D, daily. DC, MC, V.

Ninfa's. This Houston-based chain, with extensive menu, has one immense outpost in the Dallas area. Service can be inconsistent; be prepared to wait in line at peak times. 1515 Inwood; 638–6865. L, D, daily. Full bar. AE, DC, MC, V.

Raphael's. 3701 McKinney Ave., north of downtown; 521–9640. 6782 Greenville Ave., North Dallas; 692–8431. Marathon waits at the original McKinney location. Food fine, especially bean soup, chicken enchiladas, strawberry or peach sopaipillas—but you can do as well or better elsewhere. L, D, Monday through Saturday. AE, DC, MC, V.

Uncle Julio's. 4125 Lemmon Ave.; 520–6620. Festive, loud, colorful cantina setting. Classic Tex-Mex with fresh ingredients and large portions. L, D, daily. AE, DC, MC, V.

Inexpensive

La Botica. 1900 N. Haskell; 824–2005. Home-cooked Mexican food in humble surroundings. Live entertainment weekends. L, Tuesday through Friday; D, Tuesday through Saturday. No credit cards.

Chito's. 4447 Maple Ave., north of downtown; 522–9166. This small, little-known place serves really tasty, authentically home-style Tex-Mex. Nothing fancy but well worth a visit. Beer, wine. L, D, daily. MC, V.

Gonzales. 3505 W. Northwest Hwy.; 528–2960. Excellent, inexpensive home-style cooking. Try a potato-egg burrito for breakfast. Quick service. Clean, cheerful interior, or get it to go. Beer, wine. B, L, D, daily. AE, MC, V.

Herrera. 3902 Maple; 526–9427. The original Maple location is possibly the best-known Tex-Mex dive in the city. Jimmy's special and Pepe's special both offer an overwhelming sampling of Tex-Mex. There is always a line going out the door. No liquor; brown-bagging allowed. L, D, daily except Tuesday. Another location at 5427 Denton Dr., north of downtown; 630–2599. Same down-home Tex-Mex but roomier, less funky surroundings; liquor, too. Tuesday through Sunday, 11:00 A.M. to 10:00 P.M. AE, DC, MC, V.

Pepe's Fandango Mexican Restaurant and Club. 1845 Promenade in shopping center north of downtown; 680–8219. Tex-Mex served in Mexican setting. The fajitas are good. L, D, Monday through Saturday. AE, MC, V.

Pizza

Generally speaking, Dallas isn't a city for pizza lovers. Only two earn the respect of cognoscenti: Expect to wait at *Ciao,* Cedar Springs at

DALLAS AND FORT WORTH

Throckmorton; 521–0110. *Adriano's* (the Quadrangle, 2800 Routh; 871–2262) serves great, Spago-style pizzas with imaginative toppings (see "Italian").

Seafood

Surprisingly for a landlocked city, Dallas has a growing flotilla of seafood restaurants, most of them vying for preeminence in serving faultlessly fresh fish.

Expensive

Atlantic Cafe. 4546 McKinney at Knox; 559–4441. This chic, sophisticated restaurant may well serve the best seafood in town with other Continental offerings. The servings are Texas-size, the service is attentive, and the wine list is well-selected. L, D, daily except Saturday L, Sunday brunch. AE, DC, MC, V.

Café Pacific. 24 Highland Park Village, Preston Rd. at Mockingbird Ln.; 526–1170. Classy brass-and-glass decor. The food is good, featuring fresh fish, and so are the drinks, including a great Ramos gin fizz and piña colada. Very popular with the nearby Highland Park crowd, so expect a wait. L, D, daily. AE, MC, V.

Jozef's. 2719 McKinney Ave., north of downtown; 826–5560. Start with the smoked trout, which is an enjoyably out-of-the-ordinary appetizer. After that, stick with simpler choices, since Jozef's is not known for its sauces. The decor is neither here nor there: nice enough but forgettable. L, Monday through Friday; D, daily. AE, DC, MC, V.

Moderate

Atchafalaya River Cafe. 4440 Belt Line Midway; 960–6878. One of a number of new Cajun restaurants in the city, with New Orleans decor. Go for the crawfish etouffee or the stuffed trout. L, D daily. Full Bar. AE, MC, V.

Bay Street. Addison Town Center, 5348 Belt Line; 934–8502, and 8121 Walnut Hill Lane; 739–6700. Fresh and tasty seafood at affordable prices. Excellent pasta/seafood dishes such as shrimp marinara. Service helpful and steady. L, D, daily. Full bar. AE, DC, MC, V.

Oysters. 4580 Belt Line Rd. in Addison, north of far north Dallas; 386–0122. Nicely prepared oysters, shrimp, and fresh fish in a cozy, casual dining room. L, Monday through Saturday; D, daily. Full bar. AE, MC, V.

S & D Oyster Co. 2701 McKinney Ave., north of downtown; 880–0111. A crowd of dedicated regulars is always lined up outside the door, drinking beer while they await admittance to the simple, renovated warehouse. Oysters on the half shell, red snapper, boiled shrimp, and other Gulf-coast seafood are what they're here for. Don't forget about the lemon pie and cheesecake. Beer, wine, no mixed drinks. L, D, Monday through Saturday. AE, MC, V.

Inexpensive

Aw Shucks. 3601 Greenville Ave. (at Longview), in East Dallas; 821–9449. Also at 4535 Maple Ave.; 522–4498; and 3701 W. Northwest Hwy., 350–9777. These small, no frills establishments have some of the freshest, simplest seafood in the area. Beer and wine served; no liquor. L, D, daily. AE, MC, V.

Southern

Moderate

Chaise Lounge. 3010 N. Henderson; 823-1400. Hearty Southern and Cajun fare served in roadhouse setting. Corn chowder, rice pudding, panfried trout. Cajun music. D, Monday through Saturday. AE, DC, MC, V.

Inexpensive

Black-eyed Pea. 3857 Cedar Springs; 521-4580. 4814 Greenville; 361-5979. 5290 Belt Line, Addison; 233-8227. 1915 N. Central Expressway (at Park Blvd.), Plano; 423-5565. This local chain serves passable chicken-fried steak, etc. The noise level is a problem at the Belt Line and Greenville locations. L, D, daily. Full bar, Plano location requires membership. AE, DC, MC, V.

Bubba's. 6617 Hillcrest Ave., south of Lovers Ln, near Southern Methodist University (SMU); 373-6527. The bright, new slate-gray-and-lipstick-red decor is like a Salvador Dali vision. But the cooking couldn't be more old-fashioned: fried chicken, yeast rolls, down-home vegetables, and fruit cobbler. Skip Bubba's breakfast, though. No liquor. B, L, D, daily. No credit cards, but personal checks accepted.

Dixie House. 2822 McKinney Ave., north of downtown; 871-1173. Also at 3647 W. Northwest Hwy.; 353-0769. 14925 Midway, Addison; 239-5144. 6400 Gaston (at Abrams); 826-2412. These formula restaurants turn out dependable down-home southern classics. Try the squash casserole. The result is informal and popular. L, D, daily. Full bar. AE, DC, MC, V.

Rosemarie's. 1411 N. Zang; 946-4142. Chow down on simple, basic southern food and good rolls in truck-stop diner decor in Oak Cliff. No liquor. L, Monday through Friday. Personal checks.

Upper Crust. Olla Podrida Shopping Center, 12215 Coit Rd., south of LBJ Fwy.; 661-5738. The small menu changes daily and features excellent homemade offerings. Situated in an offbeat, crafts-oriented shopping center. Liquor with membership. L, Monday through Saturday; AE, DC, MC, V.

Steak

Steak chains abound in Dallas, but truly outstanding steak restaurants are surprisingly few.

Ruth's Chris Steak House. 5922 Cedar Springs Rd., near Love Field; 902-8080. Top-grade meat for those willing to pay top-grade prices. Casual atmosphere considering the tab. L, Sunday through Friday, D, daily. Full bar. AE, DC, MC, V.

Hoffbrau. 3205 Knox, North Dallas; 559-2680. Cold beer, chunky fried potatoes, and steaks pan sauteed with lemon butter are the essence of this reasonably priced menu. The decor and the jukebox are rowdy and western; the clientele always seems to be having a good time. L, D, daily. AE, DC, MC, V.

Swedish

Moderate to Expensive

Three Vikings. 4537 Cole at Knox; 559-0987. Happily, the city's only Swedish restaurant is also a fine, family-owned one. Veal Oscar, the salmon steak with dill sauce, and duck in almond sauce are proven favorites. Relaxed woods-and-plants decor. L, Tuesday-Friday, D, Monday through Saturday. AE, MC, V.

Vietnamese

Inexpensive

Mai's. 4812 Bryan St. (east of Fitzhugh Ave.), downtown; 826-9887. A small, authentic menu. Bring your own liquor. L, D, Wednesday through Sunday. MC, V.

DINING OUT IN FORT WORTH. Until a few years ago the restaurant fare in Fort Worth was largely limited to standard southwestern mainstays: Tex-Mex and barbecue. To find anything more sophisticated than that, one would need to drive 45 mi. east to Dallas. But a revitalization of the downtown area and the construction of several world-class downtown hotels has changed all that. Now it is possible to find anything from frijoles to pâté de foie gras in Fort Worth. The price classifications below follow the same dollar ranges as those for Dallas, above. All telephone numbers are area code 817.

American-International

Expensive

The Balcony. 6100 Camp Bowie; 731-3719. The Balcony is anything but innovative, but it is a place for reliable, old-style Continental cuisine: beef variations, and veal cordon bleu. L, Monday through Friday; D, Saturday; closed Sunday. All major credit cards.

Brasserie la Salle. Worthington Hotel, 200 Main St.; 870-1000. The Brasserie's offerings are eclectic classics (eggs Benedict, burgers, pasta) available around the clock. AE, DC, MC, V.

Cafe Centennial and Crystal Cactus. Hyatt Regency Hotel, 815 Main; 870-1234. The Hyatt Regency has brought a new level of ambition to downtown dining in Forth Worth with these two restaurants and has largely succeeded, with imaginative offerings along the lines of rock-lobster salad with tarragon dressing. L, daily at the Crystal Cactus and B, L, D, daily at the Cafe Centennial, AE, DC, MC, V.

The Carriage House. 5136 Camp Bowie Blvd.; 732-2873. Stick to the steak in this Fort Worth standard, and you'll be pleased you came. Venture elsewhere into the uneven menu, and you'll wonder why this is an establishment favorite. L, Monday through Friday; D, daily; Sunday brunch. AE, DC, MC, V.

Old Swiss House. 1541 Merrimac; 877-1531. This old-timer among local Continental restaurants is either constant or boring, depending on your feelings about innovation or the lack thereof. No one could complain about the reliable perfection of the service, though. D, Monday through Saturday; closed Sunday. AE, DC, MC, V.

Inexpensive

Massey's. 1805 Eighth Ave.; 924–8242. Chicken-fried steak is Massey's *raison d'être,* though you'd never catch the homespun patrons or staff using such a term. Seafood and Mexican fare are also served, but only the rankest tenderfoot would choose them. Concentrate instead on the definitive CFS and accompaniments of cream gravy and biscuits; the salad and vegetables are best forgotten. B, L, D, daily. AE, MC, V.

Barbecue

Inexpensive

Angelo's. 2533 White Settlement Rd.; 332–0357. Only Dallas's Sonny Bryan's rivals Angelo's for the ability to attract hordes of local barbecue devotees. Happily, Angelo's setting is large and relatively clean. The ribs are the thing here, so take care to arrive after 3:30 P.M., when they're served. L, D, Monday through Saturday; closed Sunday. No credit cards.

Dick's Kountry Barbecue. 316 S. Saginaw Blvd., north Fort Worth; 232–2532. Offers basic barbecued ribs, ham, beef, and staggeringly good side-orders (cole slaw, potato salad, red beans) in a log-cabin setting. L, D daily. No credit cards.

Burgers

Inexpensive

Billy Miner's. 150 W. 3rd St. (at Houston St.) 877–3301. Serves what may well be the best burger in town in casual, turn-of-the-century setting. L, D, daily. AE, MC, V.

Kincaid's. 4901 Camp Bowie; 732–2881. Unprepossessing is an understatement for the "ambience" at Kinkaid's—which is understandable enough, considering that Kincaid's is a grocery store. The specialty du jour is always the classic ½ lb. fresh meat hamburgers, and the seating is at stand-up counters or in your car. L, D, Monday through Saturday; closed Sunday. No credit cards.

Chinese

Moderate

Szechuan. 5712 Locke (near Camp Bowie); 738–7300. The decor is one cut above the standard off-the-shelf Chinese found in the rest of the city, and the spicy, if not incendiary, fare is a standout by several cuts. Full bar. L, D, Monday through Saturday, D, Sunday. AE, MC, V.

French

Expensive

Café Bowie. 4930 Camp Bowie; 735–1521. Situated in a graceful old frame house. Café Bowie consistently serves up impeccable Continental cuisine, earning it best-of-the-city consideration. Though the uncrowded seating arrangement indicates intimate conversation, the perhaps overzealous service simultaneously contraindicates it. L, Monday through Friday, D, daily; Sunday, brunch. AE, DC, MC, V.

German

Moderate

Edelweiss. 3801-A Southwest Blvd.; 738-5934. Cheese soup, sausages, and potato pancakes are served up in this beer hall, but the real attraction is—what else?—the beer (and the oompah music). D, Tuesday through Saturday; closed Sunday. AE, DC, MC, V.

Health Food

Inexpensive

The Back Porch. 2500 W. Berry; 923-0841. With its stockyard heritage, Fort Worth isn't exactly renowned as a center for the natural-foods crowd. But the Back Porch offers tasty and healthy fare to appease those who prefer to pursue health rather than cholesterol. The whole-wheat pizza, the pay-by-the-ounce salad bar, and the homemade soups are don't-miss propositions. L, D, Monday through Sunday. No credit cards.

Italian

Sardine's. 3410 Camp Bowie; 332-9937. At Sardine's, dramatically original (for Fort Worth) Italian food is enriched by live jazz. D, Monday through Sunday. Late kitchen. All major credit cards.

Mexican

Moderate

Joe T. Garcia's. 2201 N. Commerce; 626-4356. Fort Worth's most famous purveyor of Tex-Mex is an institution, not a mere restaurant. Joe T's, as familiars like to call it, is a great place for the indecisive, since there are no choices: Everybody gets "the dinner," which includes nachos, enchiladas, guacamole, rice, beans, and tortillas. The killer margarita is a must for neophytes. L, daily; D, Monday through Sunday. No credit cards.

Middle Eastern

Moderate

Hedary's. 3308 Fairfield (Ridglea Center off Camp Bowie Blvd.); 731-6961. Lebanese food in Cowtown seems unlikely enough, but Hedary's Middle Eastern food is authentic and laudable in philosophy (the menu boasts "no hot table, freezer, chemicals, or can opener"). The hummus bit-tahini (a dip of ground chickpeas, sesame seeds, lemon juice, and garlic) is a must. The setting is pleasantly relaxed. D, Tuesday through Sunday; closed Monday. All major credit cards.

Seafood

Moderate

Bill Martin's Seafood. 231 N. University; 737–4004. Also Bill Martin's Fourth Edition, 7712 S. Freeway; 293–9002. Nothing fancy here, just a wide variety of fried and broiled fish served up in a family atmosphere. These places have long been popular for their homemade hush puppies, along with fish selections ranging from fried whitefish fillets to fresh lobster. L, D, daily. AE, DC, MC, V.

Inexpensive

J&J Oyster Bar. 929 University; 335–2756. Oysters—fried or on the half shell—are the obvious attraction here. L, D, daily. AE, MC, V.

Steakhouses

Expensive

Cattlemen's. 2458 N. Main; 624–3945. Cattlemen's takes a textbook-Texan approach to dining out. The setting (including wall-to-wall cattle portraits) could hardly be more rustic, and the location is inevitable: the stockyards. Carnivores only need apply, since steak, naturally enough, is the attraction here. L, Monday through Friday; D, daily. closed Sunday. AE, DC, MC, V.

NIGHTLIFE IN DALLAS. Bar hopping is most plausible in four areas of town. The first, and far and away the most extensive, is Greenville Avenue, offering shopping during the day and dining and entertainment by night. Mockingbird Lane bisects Greenville into lower Greenville (south of Mockingbird), which is considered to be part of East Dallas, and upper Greenville (north of Mockingbird), which is considered to be part of North Dallas and home to high-tech discos such as Brio's and Etc-etera as well as restaurants and bars including T.G.I. Friday's, Cheers, and Humperdink's. Upper Greenville attracts a more flashy crowd; lower Greenville, those younger. Third is the West End/Dallas Alley in the west end historical district downtown that attracts an eclectic crowd. The fourth is the Beltline/Addison area, another gathering spot for singles.

The second is Knox Street in Highland Park, just west of North Central Expressway. Although Highland Park is preppy and yuppy, the night life is fairly relaxed.

All area codes are 214.

Andrew's. 3301 McKinney Ave. (at Hall), north of downtown; 220–0566. 14930 Midway (at Belt Line); 385–1613. Archetypal exposed-brick-and-wrought-iron decor. Specialty drinks, house salad, black-bean soup, boiled shrimp, Creole dishes, and a variety of food types for all tastes.

At the Top of the Dome. Hyatt Regency's Reunion Tower (downtown), Reunion Blvd; 651–1234. Revolves atop Reunion Tower. Casual dress. A much better idea than dinner at the overpriced Antares. Live music nightly except Sundays.

DALLAS AND FORT WORTH

Cardinal Puff's. 4615 Greenville Ave., northeast of downtown; 369-1969. Fireplace for winter months, candle-lit tables in outdoor garden for warm weather.

Club Mercedes. 7035 Greenville; 696-8686. Live music featured in this hot new club. Dance floor; late-night menu.

Etc.-etera. NorthPark East Complex, Park La. at Center; 692-5417. Popular singles club with DJ. Open 7 nights a week. Dancing to recorded top hits. Live music Sundays.

Fast & Cool Club. 3606 Greeville Ave.; 827-5544. Popular for its live music, with a Motown sound and dancing. Expect to wait in line. Open Tuesday-Saturday.

The Grape. 2808 Greenville Ave., East Dallas; 823-0133. Cozy and inviting, romantic in a funky way. Try the famed mushroom soup. Extensive wine list, as the name indicates.

Greenville Avenue Country Club. 3619 Greenville Ave., Dallas; 826-5650. The garden with a swimming pool and a bar in back is the warm-weather attraction. Best jukebox in Dallas.

Greenville Bar & Grill. 2821 Greenville Ave., Dallas; 823-6691. A historic bar with live jazz, rythym and blues, classic rock 'n' roll, monthly Dixieland, and a loud neighborhood crowd.

Hard Rock Café. 2601 McKinney Ave.; 855-5115. Popular nightclub/restaurant with occasional live music.

Improvisation Comedy Club. 9810 N. Central Expressway; 750-5868. Three comedians perform Tuesday-Sunday at this fun spot and restaurant. Headliners are generally nationally known comedians. Monday night is audition night. Also located at 4980 Beltline at Quorum; 404-8503.

Joe Miller's. 3531 McKinney Ave., north of downtown; 521-2261. This is the place if you like media hangouts or strong drinks. Three drinks and you qualify as legally dead. Recorded jazz played. Open Monday through Friday.

Knox Street Pub. 3230 Knox St., North Dallas; 526-9476. A classy pub with neighborhood clientele; jukebox. Open every night.

Longhorn Ballroom. 216 Corinth St., downtown; 428-3128. This is the real thing—a country dance hall. Live music and free dance lessons. Open Tuesday through Saturday.

Louie's. 1839 N. Henderson; 826-0505. Favored by media, advertising types, and local politicos. Casual decor; stiff drinks. Open nightly except Sunday.

Max's 403. 5500 Greenville Ave. (Old Town Shopping Center, northeast of downtown); 361-9517. Hot singles club. DJ and sound, light, and video show. Yuppy crowd. Happy hour lasts to closing on Tuesdays.

Palm Bar. Adolphus Hotel, 1321 Commerce (at Akard); 742-8100. Elegant pub atmosphere downtown. Terrific place for lunch, too.

Poor David's Pub. 1924 Greenville Ave.; 821-9891. Regional and national singers and musicians, along with an eclectic crowd, are featured at this 200-seat live music nightclub.

Prohibition Room. 703 McKinney Ave; 954-4407. Located in downtown's West End Historical District. There is live rythym and blues, and rock 'n' roll with occasional jazz. Open every Tuesday. Open seven nights a week.

Prophet Bar. 2713 Commerce; 742–2615. Artsy hangout with coffeehouse atmosphere weekdays and live contemporary music weekends. Open 7 nights a week. Very casual.

St. Martin's. 3020 Greenville Ave., East Dallas; 826–0940. A soothing, blue-toned wine bar. Live piano music Wednesday–Sunday, music and one of the city's best Sunday brunches. Open 7 nights a week. Dinners are overpriced, though.

Stoneleigh P. 2926 Maple Ave. (at Wolf), north of downtown; 871–2346. A rebuilt version of an incinerated Dallas legend. Headquarters for the self-proclaimed hip and artsy. Exceptionally good food. Notoriously eclectic jukebox. Open 7 nights a week.

TGI Friday's. Old Town Shopping Center, 5500 Greenville Ave., North Dallas; 363–5353. Also at 5150 Belt Line, Addison, north of Dallas; 386–5824. The archetypal singles bar but suitable for family meals too. Open 7 nights a week.

Venetian Room. Fairmont Hotel, Ross and Akard; 720–5227. The city's plushest showroom, with dinner and dancing. Semiformal dress.

NIGHTLIFE IN FORT WORTH. Fort Worth offers a wide diversity of night spots and watering holes, ranging from the ubiquitous American fern bar to the quintessential Texas beer joint, an institution basic to the city's sociological heritage. Visitors seeking a slice of true Texana should opt for the latter category, the best examples of which can be found in the historic stockyards area on the city's North Side. All telephones are area code 817.

The Blue Bird Night Club. 3515 Horne; 737–0453. This small, predominantly black tavern has been one of the mainstay stops on the city's nightclub circuit for quite a few years, largely because of the live jazz and rhythm and blues bands featured there.

Caravan of Dreams. 312 Houston St., downtown; 877–3000. Located in the Performing Arts Center, this new, exciting nightclub has live music five nights a week as well as frequent top jazz musicians. There is a theater on the second floor and an open-air rooftop bar full of exotic cacti.

Center Stage. Hilton Inn, Interstate 20 and Commerce St.; 335–7000. More than a fern bar, this is a horticulturist's dream, one of Fort Worth's most urbane bars. Dance floor with taped music, pool tables, video games.

Duffy's. One Tandy Center; 332–9501. This urbane downtown bar provides a good example of how diversified the city's bar scene has become in the past few years. Situated in one of the city's new architectural landmarks, this establishment could easily pass for part of midtown Manhattan or the Chicago Loop.

The Hop. 2905 W. Berry; 923–9949. A college clientele dominates this jazz-rock club, near Texas Christian University. The atmosphere is low key and less frenetic than one might expect for a college hangout. The fare includes spaghetti and pizza.

McArthur's. 3400 Bernie Anderson Road (at Camp Bowie Blvd.); 735–8851. Lounge with dance floor. D.J. music with middle-of-the-road popular sound.

Pickin' Parlour. 103 W. Exchange; 624–2592. Country-and-Western music, featuring the Hill City Cowboy Band. Tues.-Sat. No credit cards.

Ricochet. Worthington Hotel, 200 Main; 870–9885. This plush downtown nightspot is just what you might expect to find in the architectural showplace that houses it. The club caters to the expense-account set and features floor shows that have included '50s and '60s rock acts like the Shirelles and the Belmonts.

White Elephant Saloon. 106 E. Exchange Ave.; 624–1887. This stockyards bar, more than 100 years old, offers patrons a chance to drink and dance in an atmosphere that looks like something from the Gunsmoke set. The bar frequently has live country bands.

INDEX

Acton St. Park, 76
Addison, 42
Age of Steam Railroad
  Museum, 82
Air travel, 53–54
Amon Carter Museum, 43, 83
Amon Carter Stadium, 52
Arlington KOA, 76
Arlington Stadium, 42, 77
Arts and crafts, 89
Auto racing, 78

Bachman Lake, 42
Baseball, 77
Basketball, 77
Biblical Arts Center, 82
Bicycling, 77
Bob Hope Theater, 87
Bonham St. Park, 76
Bowling, 78
British visitors' information,
  3–4
Bryan's (John Neely), cabin, 40,
  79–80
Bus travel, 54, 63

Camping, 75–76
  general information, 12–13
Car travel, 54–55, 64; rental, 55
Casa Manana Theater, 52, 88
Cattlemen's Museum, 85
Cedar Creek Lake, 75

Children's activities, 73
Cleburne St. Park, 76
Climate, 4
Costs, 5–6
Cotton Bowl, 42, 65, 66, 68, 78

Dallas Aquarium, 82
Dallas Arboretum and Botanical
  Society, 70
Dallas Black Dance Theatre, 87
Dallas Chamber Music Society,
  86
Dallas Civic Garden Center, 70
Dallas Civic Music Association,
  86
Dallas Classic Guitar Society,
  86
Dallas Farmer's Market, 89
Dallas/Fort Worth Regional
  Airport, 40, 42, 46, 53–54,
  62–63
Dallas Grand Opera
  Association, 86
Dallas Jazz Society, 86
Dallas Library, 46
Dallas Market Center, 42, 43, 89
Dallas Marsalis Park and Zoo,
  42
Dallas Museum of Art, 46, 81
Dallas Museum of Natural
  History, 81–82
Dallas Opera, 86

INDEX

Dallas Repertory Theatre, 87
Dallas Shakespeare Festival, 87
Dallas Summer Musicals, 87
Dallas Symphony Orchestra, 85
Dallas Theater Center, 87
Dance, 86–87. *See also specific companies*
Dealey Plaza, 41, 80
DeGolyer Estate, 80
Dining. *See* Restaurants
Dinosaur Valley St. Park, 76
Drinking laws, 11

Eagle Mountain Lake, 74
Eisenhower Birthplace, 76
Eisenhower St. Park, 76
Emergency telephone numbers, 55

Facts & figures, 1–2
Fire Museum of Texas, 42
Fishin' Place, The, 71–72
Fishing, 73–75
Flea markets, 75, 89
Food and drink, 31–38. *See also* Restaurants
Football, 42, 77
Forest Park, 52, 69
Forest Park Train, 69, 73
Fort Richardson St. Park, 76
Fort Worth Art Museum, 83
Fort Worth Ballet, 87
Fort Worth Botanic Gardens, 52, 69
Fort Worth Japanese Garden, 52, 69
Fort Worth Museum of Science and History, 45, 73, 84
Fort Worth Nature Center and Refuge, 68
Fort Worth Opera, 86
Fort Worth Stockyards, 52, 78
Fort Worth Symphony Orchestra, 86
Fort Worth Theatre, 88
Fort Worth Water Gardens, 70
Fort Worth Zoological Park, 52, 69, 73
Free events, 66–67

Galleria, 42, 77, 88
Gardens, 69–70
Golf, 78
Governor Hogg Shrine, 76
Greenville Avenue, 42
Greenville Avenue Theatre, 87

Hall of State, 82
Handicapped travelers, 13–14
Hell's Half Acre, 47
Hip Pocket Theatre, 88
Historic sites, 78–79. *See also specific sites*
Holidays, 11
Horseback riding, 77
Hotels and motels, 55–62
  Dallas area, 57–61
  Dallas/Fort Worth Airport Mid-Cities area, 56–57
  Fort Worth area, 61–62
  general information, 7–9, 55–56
Hours of business, 11

Ice skating, 77
International Museum of Culture, 83
International Theatrical Arts Society, 86
International Wildlife Park, 42, 72, 73

Joe Pool Lake, 74
Johnnie High Country Music Revue, 86

Kennedy, John F., Memorial Plaza, 42, 80
Kimbell Art Museum, 45, 84
KowBell Ranch, 73, 78

Lake Arlington, 74

INDEX

Lake Benbrook, 74
Lake Granbury, 74
Lake Grapevine, 74
Lake Lavon, 74
Lake Lewisville, 74
Lake Ray Hubbard, 75
Lakes, 73–75. *See also specific lakes*
Lake Tawakoni, 75
Lake Texoma, 75
Lake Whitney, 75
Lake Worth, 75
Libraries, 81
Lifestyle, 15–19
Local time, 11
Log Cabin Village, 52, 79

Mail & postage, 11
Majestic Theatre, 87–88
Maps
  Dallas downtown, 41
  Dallas/Fort Worth area, 48–49
  Fort Worth, 50–51
  greater Dallas, 44–45
  Texas, viii–ix
Margo Jones Theatre, 87
Motoring hints, 6–7
Mountain Creek Lake, 74
Museums and galleries, 46, 68, 81–85. *See also specific sites*
Museum of African-American Art and Culture, 82–83
Music, 85–86. *See also* Nightlife
Music Hall, 68, 85

Neiman-Marcus, 43, 88
Nightlife
  Dallas, 106–108
  Fort Worth, 108–109
Noble Planetarium, 84
NorthPark Shopping Center, 42, 89

Oak Cliff, 42, 80
Old City Park, 68, 79

Old Tige's Dallas Firefighters Museum, 82
Omni-Max Theatre, 73, 84
Opera, 86

Packing & clothing, 4–5
Parks, 67–69. *See also specific sites and State Parks*
Pate Museum of Transportation, 85
Pedestrian hints, 64
Penny Whistle Park, 73
Pets, 7
Plaza of the Americas, 77
Polo, 77
Population, 16
Possum Kingdom Lake, 75, 76
Prestonwood Town Center, 42, 77, 88

Ranches, 73
Restaurants
  Dallas, 90–103
  Fort Worth, 103–106
  general information, 90–92
Reunion Arena, 77
Reunion Tower, 80
River Ridge Pavilion, 71
Rodeo, 77

Sandy Lake Park, 72–73
Science Place, 82
Scott, William Edrington, Theatre, 88
Seasonal events, 65–66
Senior-citizen & student discounts, 10–11
Shakespeare festival, 87, 88
Shopping
  Dallas, 88–90
  Fort Worth, 90
Sid Richardson Collection of Western Art, 83
Six Flags Over Texas, 70–71, 73
Southern Methodist University, 42

INDEX

Southwestern Opera Theatre, 86
Sports, 42–43, 76–78
 general information, 12
Stage, 87–88. *See also specific companies and theaters*
Stage No. 1, 87
State Fair Coliseum, 68
State Fair Park, 67–68
State Parks, 76. *See also specific parks*
Sundance Square, 52, 79, 90
Swiss Avenue, 80

Tandy Archaeological Museum, 85
Tandy Subway, 63
Tarrant County Convention Center, 47
Taxis, 63–64
Telephones, 55
Tennis, 77, 78
Texas Boys Choir, 86
Texas Christian University, 52
Texas Sports Hall of Fame, 42
Texas Stadium, 42, 78
Texas State Fair Grounds. *See State Fair Park*
Thanks-Giving Square, 68
Theater. *See Stage*
Theatre Three, 87
Theme parks and amusement centers, 13, 70–73. *See also specific sites*

Thistle Hill, 79
Tipping, 9–10
Tourist Information for Dallas/Fort Worth, 64–65
 for Texas, 2–3
Tours, 67
Traders Village, 75, 89
Trailers, 7, 12–13
Train travel, 54
Transportation, 53–55, 62–64. *See also specific means*
Trinity Park, 52, 69
Trinity River, 39, 46, 47, 52
Trip planning, 2
Tyler State Park, 76

Union Station, 42, 80

Valley View Mall, 42
Van Zandt Cottage, 79

Wax Museum of the Southwest, 42, 72
West End Historic District, 80
West Fork Ranch, 73
Wet 'n Wild, 42, 71
White Rock Lake Park, 42, 75
Will Rogers Memorial Center, 52, 78
Will Rogers Statue, 79
Wrestling, 78

Zoos, 69

Fodor's Travel Guides

U.S. Guides

Alaska
American Cities
The American South
Arizona
Atlantic City & the New Jersey Shore
Boston
California
Cape Cod
Carolinas & the Georgia Coast
Chesapeake
Chicago
Colorado
Dallas & Fort Worth
Disney World & the Orlando Area
The Far West
Florida
Greater Miami, Fort Lauderdale, Palm Beach
Hawaii
Hawaii *(Great Travel Values)*
Houston & Galveston
I-10: California to Florida
I-55: Chicago to New Orleans
I-75: Michigan to Florida
I-80: San Francisco to New York
I-95: Maine to Miami
Las Vegas
Los Angeles, Orange County, Palm Springs
Maui
New England
New Mexico
New Orleans
New Orleans *(Pocket Guide)*
New York City
New York City *(Pocket Guide)*
New York State
Pacific North Coast
Philadelphia
Puerto Rico *(Fun in)*
Rockies
San Diego
San Francisco
San Francisco *(Pocket Guide)*
Texas
United States of America
Virgin Islands (U.S. & British)
Virginia
Waikiki
Washington, DC
Williamsburg, Jamestown & Yorktown

Foreign Guides

Acapulco
Amsterdam
Australia, New Zealand & the South Pacific
Austria
The Bahamas
The Bahamas *(Pocket Guide)*
Barbados *(Fun in)*
Beijing, Guangzhou & Shanghai
Belgium & Luxembourg
Bermuda
Brazil
Britain *(Great Travel Values)*
Canada
Canada *(Great Travel Values)*
Canada's Maritime Provinces
Cancún, Cozumel, Mérida, The Yucatán
Caribbean
Caribbean *(Great Travel Values)*
Central America
Copenhagen, Stockholm, Oslo, Helsinki, Reykjavik
Eastern Europe
Egypt
Europe
Europe *(Budget)*
Florence & Venice
France
France *(Great Travel Values)*
Germany
Germany *(Great Travel Values)*
Great Britain
Greece
Holland
Hong Kong & Macau
Hungary
India
Ireland
Israel
Italy
Italy *(Great Travel Values)*
Jamaica *(Fun in)*
Japan
Japan *(Great Travel Values)*
Jordan & the Holy Land
Kenya
Korea
Lisbon
Loire Valley
London
London *(Pocket Guide)*
London *(Great Travel Values)*
Madrid
Mexico
Mexico *(Great Travel Values)*
Mexico City & Acapulco
Mexico's Baja & Puerto Vallarta, Mazatlán, Manzanillo, Copper Canyon
Montreal
Munich
New Zealand
North Africa
Paris
Paris *(Pocket Guide)*
People's Republic of China
Portugal
Province of Quebec
Rio de Janeiro
The Riviera *(Fun on)*
Rome
St. Martin/St. Maarten
Scandinavia
Scotland
Singapore
South America
South Pacific
Southeast Asia
Soviet Union
Spain
Spain *(Great Travel Values)*
Sweden
Switzerland
Sydney
Tokyo
Toronto
Turkey
Vienna
Yugoslavia

Special-Interest Guides

Bed & Breakfast Guide: North America
1936...On the Continent
Royalty Watching
Selected Hotels of Europe
Selected Resorts and Hotels of the U.S.
Ski Resorts of North America
Views to Dine by around the World